LAW, CRIME AND LAW ENFORCEMENT

NEW DEVELOPMENTS IN HUMAN RIGHTS

LAW, CRIME AND LAW ENFORCEMENT

Additional books in this series can be found on Nova's website under the Series tab.

Additional E-books in this series can be found on Nova's website under the E-books tab.

LAW, CRIME AND LAW ENFORCEMENT

NEW DEVELOPMENTS IN HUMAN RIGHTS

JENNIFER M. BAUER
AND
COLIN P. DAVIES
EDITORS

Nova Science Publishers, Inc.
New York

For permission to use material from this book please contact us:
Telephone 631-231-7269; Fax 631-231-8175
Web Site: http://www.novapublishers.com

NOTICE TO THE READER

Additional color graphics may be available in the e-book version of this book.

Library of Congress Cataloging-in-Publication Data

New developments in human rights / editors, Jennifer M. Bauer and Colin P. Davies.
p. cm.
Includes index.
ISBN 978-1-61324-316-9 (hardcover)
1. Civil rights--United States. I. Bauer, Jennifer M. II. Davies, Colin P.
KF4750.N365 2011
342.7308'5--dc22

2011010133

Published by Nova Science Publishers, Inc. † New York

CONTENTS

PREFACE*

This book presents current research in the study of basic human rights, with a particular focus on the crimes against human rights and the laws which protect human rights. Topics discussed include terrorism and Miranda rights; characteristics of women who withdraw from the protection order process and their reason for withdrawal; judicial activity concerning enemy combatant detainees; the law and military policy on same-sex behavior and the Violence against Women Act.

Chapter 1 - Among research on intimate partner violence, little attention has been given to the characteristics of victims who withdraw from the protection order process and how these characteristics may be related to their decisions for withdrawal. The present study is an initial exploratory attempt to address this gap in the literature. Fifty-seven women who were in the process of withdrawing a protection order against a male intimate partner were surveyed in the present analysis. Findings suggest that women who were under age 40 were more likely to withdraw protection orders for some family issue (i.e., children missed defendant) than were women who were older, while those who were employed and those who were 40 years or older were more likely to withdraw protection orders because of some concrete change that had occurred (i.e., defendant receiving counseling). Implications of these findings are discussed and suggestions are offered for future research.

Chapter 2 - The Fifth Amendment to the United States Constitution provides in part that "No person ... shall be compelled in any criminal case to be a witness against himself, nor be deprived of life, liberty, or property, without due process

---

* Versions of these chapters were also published in the *Journal of Current Law Issues in Crime, Law and Law Enforcement,* Volume 3, Numbers 1-4, edited by Frank Columbus, published by Nova Science Publishers, Inc. They were submitted for appropriate modifications in an effort to encourage wider dissemination of research.

of law." In Miranda v. Arizona, the Supreme Court declared that statements of an accused, given during a custodial interrogation, could not be introduced in evidence in criminal proceedings against him, unless he were first advised of his rights and waived them. In Dickerson v. United States, the Court held that the Miranda exclusionary rule was constitutionally grounded and could not be replaced by a statutory provision making all voluntary confessions admissible. In New York v. Quarles, the Court recognized a "limited" "public safety" exception to Miranda, but has not defined the exception further. The lower federal courts have construed the exception narrowly in cases involving unwarned statements concerning the location of a weapon possibly at hand at the time of an arrest.

Chapter 3 - As part of the conflict with Al Qaeda and the Taliban, the United States has captured and detained numerous persons believed to have been part of or associated with enemy forces. Over the years, federal courts have considered a multitude of petitions by or on behalf of suspected belligerents challenging aspects of U.S. detention policy. Although the Supreme Court has issued definitive rulings concerning several legal issues raised in the conflict with Al Qaeda and the Taliban, many others remain unresolved, with some the subject of ongoing litigation.

This report discusses major judicial opinions concerning suspected enemy belligerents detained in the conflict with Al Qaeda and the Taliban. The report addresses all Supreme Court decisions concerning enemy combatants. It also discusses notable circuit court opinions addressing issues of ongoing relevance to U.S. detention policy. The report also addresses a few notable decisions by federal district courts that are the subject of ongoing *habeas* litigation. Finally, it describes a few federal court rulings in criminal cases involving persons who were either involved in the 9/11 attacks or were captured abroad by U.S. forces during operations against Al Qaeda, the Taliban, and associated entities.

Chapter 4 - In 1993, new laws and regulations pertaining to homosexuality and U.S. military service came into effect reflecting a compromise in policy. This compromise, colloquially referred to as "don't ask, don't tell," holds that the presence in the armed forces of persons who demonstrate a propensity or intent to engage in same-sex acts would create an unacceptable risk to the high standards of morale, good order and discipline, and unit cohesion which are the essence of military capability. Under this policy, but not the law, service members are not to be asked about nor allowed to discuss their "same-sex orientation." The law itself does not prevent service members from being asked about their sexuality. This compromise notwithstanding, the issue has remained politically contentious. Prior to the 1993 compromise, the number of individuals discharged for homosexuality was generally declining. Since that time, the number of discharges for same-sex conduct has generally increased until 2001. However, analysis of these data shows no statistically significant difference in discharge rates for these two periods.

Chapter 5 - The Violence Against Women and Department of Justice Reauthorization Act of 2005 (VAWA 2005) (P.L. 109-162) was enacted on January 5, 2006. Among other things, VAWA 2005 reauthorized existing VAWA programs and created many new programs. The act encourages collaboration among law enforcement, judicial personnel, and public and private service providers to victims of domestic and sexual violence; increases public awareness of domestic violence; addresses the special needs of victims of domestic and sexual violence, including the elderly, disabled, children, youth, and individuals of ethnic and racial communities; authorizes long-term and transitional housing for victims; makes some provisions gender-neutral; and requires studies and reports on the effectiveness of approaches used for certain grants in combating violence.

In: New Developments in Human Rights
Editors: J. M. Bauer and C. P. Davies
ISBN 978-1-61324-316-9

Chapter 1

CHARACTERISTICS OF WOMEN WHO WITHDRAW FROM THE PROTECTION ORDER PROCESS AND THEIR DECISIONS FOR WITHDRAWAL

***Marie Mele*[1*], *C. James Roberts*[2] *and Loreen Wolfer*[2]**
[1]Monmouth University, New Jersey, U. S.
[2]The University of Scranton, Pennsylvania, U. S.

ABSTRACT

Among research on intimate partner violence, little attention has been given to the characteristics of victims who withdraw from the protection order process and how these characteristics may be related to their decisions for withdrawal. The present study is an initial exploratory attempt to address this gap in the literature. Fifty-seven women who were in the process of withdrawing a protection order against a male intimate partner were surveyed in the present analysis. Findings suggest that women who were under age 40 were more likely to withdraw protection orders for some family issue (i.e., children missed defendant) than were women who were older, while those who were employed and those who were 40 years or older were more likely to withdraw protection orders because of some concrete change that had

* Contact author: Marie Mele Department of Criminal Justice Monmouth University West Long Branch, NJ 07764 732.571.7567 mmele@monmouth.edu

occurred (i.e., defendant receiving counseling). Implications of these findings are discussed and suggestions are offered for future research.

INTRODUCTION

The difficulties women face in ending abusive intimate partner relationships have been well documented by anecdotal and empirical research. Studies have suggested a number of factors that inhibit women's decisions to leave abusive partners, including inadequate criminal justice responses (Davis, 1998; Epstein, 1999), lack of social support (Bates and Toro, 1999; Short et al., 2000), economic dependency on their partner (Johnson, 1992; Tan and Davidson, 1992), self-blame (Pape and Arias, 2000), a sense of commitment to the relationship (Towns and Adams, 2000), and fear of retaliation from their partner (Langford, 1996). Although many women eventually leave abusive partners, their first attempts are often unsuccessful (Herbert, Silver, and Ellard, 1991; Campbell et al., 1994). It has been estimated that the average woman makes up to five attempts to leave her abusive partner before she successfully ends the relationship (Okun, 1986). Even after ending the relationship, many women still endure threats of physical harm, harassment and stalking (Wilson, Johnson and Daly, 1995; Kurz, 1996). Due to the cyclical nature of intimate partner violence, about half of all women who leave an abusive relationship ultimately reunite with their abusive partner (Schutte, Malouff and Doyle, 1988).

Several studies have sought to identify common characteristics among women who remain with or return to abusive partners. Strube and Barbour (1984), for example, found that married women and Caucasian women were more likely than unmarried women and non-Caucasian women to return to their abusive partners. The authors suggested that married women may be more committed to saving the relationship because of the difficulties associated with divorce. They also suggested that the finding related to race may reflect the lower likelihood of minority women to marry their intimate partners. Research also suggests that a woman's age may influence her decision to stay with an abusive partner. Wilke and Vinton (2005) found that older women (above age 45) were more likely than younger women to remain with their abusive partners. The authors suggested that younger women may have greater knowledge about intimate partner violence and the services available to help them protect themselves from abusive partners, while older women may be more accepting of relationships based on male dominance or may fear losing their partner without the prospect of remarriage.

Although several studies have attempted to identify personality traits of women who stay with or return to abusive partners, after a review of the literature, Rhodes and McKenzie (1998) concluded that, "a single personality trait or group of characteristics may not be found that can explain the tenacity of a battered woman in remaining with her violent partner" (396). It is more likely that situational factors, such as financial resources and social support, influence women's decisions to remain with abusive partners more so than any element of their personality. Further, a woman's decision to stay with an abusive partner may not be the result of a single situational factor, but rather the combination of several such variables.

Women who do choose to end an abusive relationship may decide to obtain a protection (or restraining) order. Among women who report their victimization to the police, about one third obtains a protection order against their abuser (Hathaway et al., 2000). A protection order not only offers victims an avenue for legal action against the abuser, it also gives victims the opportunity to separate themselves from the abuser and take the necessary steps to establish their independence. Many women who apply for a protection order, however, do not follow through with the entire process. This reluctance to follow through may be due to an emotional attachment to the abuser (the stronger the attachment, the less likely women are to follow through with the protection order) or fear of retaliation from the abuser (Zoellner et al., 2000; DeMaris and Swinford, 1996). The severity of abuse may also influence the victim's decision to follow through with the protection order process: the more severe the abuse, the less likely the victim is to follow through (Fernandez, Iwamoto and Muscat, 1997).

It is clear that much of the existing research focuses on why women remain with or return to abusive partners. With few exceptions (i.e., Zoellner et al., 2000; DeMaris and Swinford, 1996), researchers have not sought to understand why women fail to follow through with the protection order process, regardless of whether they return to their abusive partners. This omission seems to imply that the same reasons women withdraw protection orders would be the same reasons they return to their partner. Among the limited studies of protection order withdrawal, there does not seem to be the recognition that women may withdraw a protection order because some aspect of the circumstance has concretely changed, thereby leading some women to believe that they no longer need the protection order. In addition, little is known about the characteristics of women who withdraw from the protection order process and how these characteristics may be related to their reasons for withdrawal.

The present study is an initial exploratory attempt to address this gap in the literature. Specifically, the study explores: 1) common characteristics among women who withdraw from the protection order process, 2) whether these characteristics are related to their reasons for withdrawal; and 3) whether specific forms of social support may have prevented women of different characteristics from withdrawing their protection orders.

METHODS

This study focuses on women in Blair County, Pennsylvania who were in the process of withdrawing a protection from abuse order that was filed against a male intimate partner. Blair County is located in central Pennsylvania and has a population of roughly 129,000 people. The county is predominantly Caucasian (98%), the median household income is $32,861, and the median age is 40 years. The majority (66%) of county residents has a high school education or less, 20% have some college education, and 14% have a college degree or more (U.S. Census, 2000).

In the state of Pennsylvania, victims of intimate partner violence can apply for a protection from abuse (PFA) order. A PFA is a civil court order that instructs the defendant not to harm or have contact with the plaintiff. A PFA may also prohibit the defendant from having contact with the plaintiff's children or family members. A PFA may be granted to people who are assaulted or threatened by a current or former intimate partner (regardless of whether they reside together), a co-parent, a current or former spouse and any other family member (i.e., parent, sibling, children, etc.).

While every county has a slightly different process for obtaining a PFA, it usually starts with the plaintiff filing a petition with the Court of Common Pleas that describes the abuse they have suffered and the protection they are seeking. Next, an emergency or ex-parte hearing is held, during which time a judge will either grant the plaintiff a temporary PFA and set a date for a final PFA hearing (usually held within 10 days of the initial hearing) or deny the temporary PFA. At the final PFA hearing, a judge decides whether to grant a final order, which lasts up to 18 months and, under certain circumstances, can be extended. At any point in the process, a plaintiff can withdraw his/her request for a PFA by filing a PFA withdrawal order. Once this order is filed, a withdraw petition hearing is held. At this hearing, a judge decides whether to vacate the PFA. If the withdrawal order is granted, the PFA is immediately vacated. A plaintiff can also decide not to seek a final PFA at the final hearing.

Women who were in the process of withdrawing a PFA against a male intimate partner were the focus of the present study. Fifty-nine women were surveyed as they left a final PFA hearing or a withdraw petition hearing. Survey responses reveal that two women only reported abusive actions towards children (and not themselves); therefore, these two women were omitted from the analysis. This left a final sample size of 57 women. Respondents were surveyed on their reasons for obtaining a PFA and their reasons for withdrawing a PFA. Surveys also included questions on services that may have prevented respondents from failing to complete the protection order process and demographic questions about the individuals (bringing the total number of survey items to nine). Prior to their participation, respondents were informed about the purpose of the survey, and told that their participation was voluntary and that their identities would remain confidential. Respondents were not compensated for their participation.

All women attending a final PFA hearing or withdraw hearing between July 2005 and January 2006 agreed to participate in the survey. The willingness of these women to participate in the survey may be a reflection of the positive, trusting relationship most had with the victim advocates who administered it. Furthermore, participants in this study were given the option of either an oral administration or written administration of the survey. The oral administration of the survey entailed victim advocates both reading and marking responses to the questions contained within, while the written administration entailed victims reading the questions and marking responses on their own. The average time needed to complete the survey was less than five minutes, with the vast majority of participants opting to complete it on their own in the presence of a victim advocate who was available to answer any questions. Participants were surveyed before leaving the courtroom and out of the presence of abusive partners who were sometimes waiting outside. The survey instrument administered in this study had been developed and used previously by victim advocates from the Blair County Domestic Abuse Project to assess the needs of battered women. The development of this survey was based on insights gained from these advocates' many interactions with victims of abuse, as well as their participation in professional conferences and seminars on intimate partner violence.

The survey instrument administered in the present study included 13 different reasons a woman might withdraw a PFA and included a 14th "other" category where women could write in a different response if none of the 13 presented were applicable. Following Johnson's (1992) lead, and the approach taken in our previous research (Roberts et al., 2008) these individual reasons were organized along domains.

The domains we used and their corresponding individual choices included:

Resources:	PFA withdrawn because the victim needs the defendant for food, shelter, healthcare, etc.
Emotional attachment:	PFA withdrawn because the defendant promises to change and/or the victim is no longer afraid of the defendant.
Concrete change:	PFA withdrawn because the defendant is attending counseling or rehabilitation, the defendant is moving, the victim is moving, and/or the individuals are separating or divorcing.
Family issues:	PFA withdrawn because the defendant is missed by the children or the victim is pregnant with the defendant's child.
Bureaucratic issues:	PFA withdrawn because the victim failed to appear at the court hearing and/or the victim is dissatisfied with the legal system.

We treated the defendant's *promise* to change and actually *attending* counseling or rehabilitation as different. A "promise" has no concrete action associated with it; therefore, if the victim accepts it, that acceptance is based on the victim's emotional faith in the defendant. This emotional tie is a common observation noted in the literature. However, a defendant who is actually attending counseling is showing steps that may lead to actual behavior change. Of course, the defendant may only be attending counseling due to a court order (as opposed to recognition for the need to change or a desire to change); however, from a victim's perspective, regardless of the motivation for attendance, the *result* of attendance may be behavior change. In other words, the victim may believe that by attending counseling (willingly or not), the defendant is going to change his behavior; and, it is the belief that stems from that concrete action that leads the victim to withdraw the protection order.

The main individual characteristics of the women included in this study were their age (under age 40, age 40 or older), whether they had children, whether they were employed, whether they had at least some high school education or high school degree compared to whether they had at least some college education, and their reason for filing this particular PFA. Some of these characteristics (for example, age) had more categories than are represented in this analysis. That is because, due to issues with some small cell sizes, many of the analyses needed to be conducted on 2X2 tables, which lead to the collapsing of some of these characteristics into only two categories.

FINDINGS

Although the sample is small, it suggests some common characteristics among women who withdraw protection from abuse orders. Consistent with the demographics of Blair County, the majority of the women in the sample were white (96.4%). In addition, 73.4% of the women were under age 40, almost two-thirds (67.3%) had one or more children and 69.6% had a high school education or less. Almost one third of the sample was not employed (31.5%); and, only three respondents earned more than $30,000 a year. The two most common reasons women reported for obtaining a PFA were some type of physical abuse such as pushing, slapping, punching, kicking, etc. (59.6%) and a threat of serious bodily injury made to the plaintiff by the defendant (38.6%). Responses falling into the "other" category included defendant's "erratic/unpredictable" behavior, defendant's "harassing" behavior, loved ones and friends pressuring plaintiff to file PFA, and landlord threatening eviction if plaintiff did not file PFA.

The most common reason women withdrew protection orders was that they no longer feared the defendant (35.1%), followed by a tie between the defendant attending counseling/rehabilitation and the defendant promising to change (28.1% each). Responses falling into the "other" category included plaintiff needing defendant for protection against new boyfriend, plaintiff realizing that obtaining a PFA was a "mistake" and that they had been pressured into filing it, plaintiff's desire to start over, and PFA order getting in the way of child custody. When grouping individual reasons for withdrawal into domains, the most common domain response was a tie between emotional attachment and some type of concrete change (49.1% each). For a more thorough analysis of these domains, please see Roberts et al., (2008).

The primary goal of this paper was to see whether reasons for withdrawing protection orders varied by individual characteristics of the women. The only characteristics which had any statistically significant effect on reason for PFA withdrawal were age and employment status. With regards to age, as indicated in Table 2, those under the age of 40 were much more likely to withdraw protection orders for some family reason than those who were older. While no respondents who were 40 or older withdrew for family reasons, almost one-third (31.7%) of those younger than 40 did ($p<.05$).

Table 1. Descriptive Statistics of Sample and PFA Experiences

	%	n
Reason Obtained PFA		
Physical abuse	59.6	34
Sexual abuse	0	0
Threat of serious bodily injury	38.6	22
False imprisonment, restraint	3.5	2
Physical or sexual abuse of child	3.5	2
Other	17.5	10
Individual Reason Withdrew PFA		
Needed resources of defendant (e.g., money, shelter, etc.)	12.3	7
Defendant promised to change	28.1	16
Defendant threatened to continue abuse	0	0
Defendant attending counseling / rehabilitation	28.1	16
Defendant missed by children	15.8	9
Defendant is moving	3.5	2
Victim is moving	10.5	6
Victim is no longer afraid	35.1	20
Victim failed to appear in court hearing	0	0
Victim is pregnant with defendant's child	7.0	4
Victim dissatisfied with legal system	1.8	1
Parties separating / divorcing	8.8	5
Family illness	0	0
Other	29.8	17
Withdrawal of PFAs – Domains		
Resources	12.3	7
Emotional attachment	49.1	28
Concrete change	49.1	28
Family reasons	22.8	13
Bureaucratic	1.8	1

Table 2. Relationship between Age and PFA Withdrawal due to Family Reasons

Withdrew Due to Family Reason	Age****		Age: No Children		Age: **** Children	
	Under 40	40 and Older	Under 40	40 and Older	Under 40	40 and Older
Yes	31.7% (13)		27.3% (3)		34.5% (10)	
No	68.3% (28)	100% (15)	72.7% (8)	100% (7)	65.5% (19)	100% (8)

The second age effect related to the concrete change domain. Those who were 40 or older were more likely to withdraw a PFA for some type of concrete change (73.3%) than were those who were younger (41.5%, p<.05, Table 3).

Table 3. Relationship between Age and Reason for PFA Withdrawal

	Age	
Withdrew due to Concrete Change	Under 40	40 and Older
Yes	41.5% (17)	73.3% (11)
No	58.5% (24)	26.7% (4)

p<.05.

Employment status also seemed to relate to reason for protection order withdrawal. Those who were employed were more likely to withdraw protection orders because of some "concrete change" that had occurred. Almost two-thirds (62.2%) of those who were employed withdrew their PFA due to some concrete change, compared to 17.6% of those who were unemployed (p=.01, Table 4).

Table 4. Relationship between Employment Status and Reason for PFA Withdrawal

	Employed	
Withdrew due to Concrete Change**	No	Yes
Yes	17.6% (3).	62.2% (23)
No	82.4% (14)	37.8% (14)

When asked what type of help or assistance could have prevented the respondents from withdrawing the PFA and returning to the defendant, 89.5% of them reported that there was no assistance that could have prevented them from withdrawing the PFA. Age, having children, employment status and educational level all had no statistically significant effect on any reported factors that could have prevented PFA withdrawal.

DISCUSSION AND CONCLUSION

As mentioned previously, the present study was an initial, exploratory attempt to better understand the characteristics of women who withdraw from the protection order process and how these characteristics may be related to their reasons for withdrawal. Among the sample of 57 women included in this study, most were young (under age 40), most had little education beyond high school, most were employed but earned little money (less than $30,000 a year), and most had one or more children. The analyses yielded several interesting findings when examining the relationship between these characteristics and reasons for withdrawing PFAs.

Contrary to some previous studies, these women were not to withdraw PFAs because they feared retaliation from the defendant (Zoellner et al., 2000; DeMaris and Swinford, 1996). Among our sample of women, the most common reason they withdrew their PFA was because they were no longer afraid of the defendant, the defendant had promised to change, or because the defendant was attending counseling. However, we agree with Rhodes and McKenzie (1998) that women return to abusers because of a combination of factors, therefore; we grouped a number of these factors into domains based on various themes (Roberts et al, 2008). Those groupings suggest that these women were most likely to withdraw their PFAs because of some concrete change in their situation (e.g. the defendant was in counseling or one or more parties was moving) or some level of emotional attachment to the defendant (e.g. the defendant promising to change or the plaintiff no longer fearing the defendant).

There were very few significant differences in domain related reasons for PFA withdraw based on individual characteristics of these women. Only age of the defendant and employment status had any statistically significant effect on why these women withdrew their PFAs. Women under 40 were more likely to withdraw a PFA for a family reason. The reluctance of women to follow through with the protection order process may be suggestive of an attachment issue (see DeMaris and Swinford, 1996; Zoellner et al., 2000) or a support issue (see

Johnson, 1988; Bates and Toro, 1999). However, it may also be an indication of lack of faith in the way agencies respond to intimate partner violence when children enter the equation. According to DeVoe and Smith (2003), while victim advocates place an emphasis on "empowering" battered women, child protective services (CPS) agencies typically focus on the safety and well-being of the child, which may translate into removal of children from the home. Removal of children from the home is especially likely if their exposure to violence is considered a form of child maltreatment (i.e., neglect, emotional abuse, etc.). In other words, the reluctance of battered women to seek help for abuse, or in the case of those in our sample, the reluctance of women to follow through with the protection order process, may arise from their fear of losing their children.

Findings from this study also revealed statistically significant relationships between the variables age and employment and the domain "concrete change." Again, those who were employed and those who were age 40 or over were more likely to withdraw protection orders because of some concrete change that had occurred, such as defendant receiving counseling. Interestingly, past research (i.e., Frisch and MacKenzie, 1991; Johnson, 1992) indicates that women who are unemployed or are less educated are less likely to leave an abusive relationship due to lack of resources, suggesting a type of economic dependency on the abuser. The opposite implication then is that employed and educated women leave because they can afford to. However, our findings suggest that this may be more complicated than previously thought. There's a noticeable trend that those who are employed are *not* leaving; they are withdrawing their protection orders and, while it is unknown if they are actually *returning* to their abusers, they do at least appear to have some faith that the abuser will change his behavior because he is actively seeking treatment for it.

In considering the above findings, one must keep in mind limitations of the present study. The most notable limitation was the failure to include a comparison group of women who followed through with the protection order process. The inclusion of such a comparison group would allow researchers to determine whether the characteristics of those who withdraw PFAs are unique to this subgroup or whether they are common to the general population of women who obtain PFAs. Further, since the sample of women in the present study was mostly young and mostly white, it is unclear whether the findings are generalizable to other populations. Other limitations, such as the small sample size, which placed limitations on the analyses that could be performed, should also be addressed in future research.

There is a great need for more extensive studies of PFA withdrawal, since much of the existing research focuses on reasons why women stay with and/or return to abusive partners. Further, increased and more extensive studies of PFA withdrawal will allow researchers to determine whether the characteristics of women who withdraw protection orders are similar to or different than those of women who stay with and/or return to abusive partners. It may well be determined that these are three distinctly different situations, involving three distinctly different groups of women. Such a determination should aid practitioners in better attending to the needs of battered women. Additionally, researchers must make an effort to determine whether there are distinct groupings of factors or variables that influence decisions to stay with abusive partners, return to abusive partners, or withdraw protection orders. Again, the consideration of domains such as those examined in the present study may be particularly useful in this type of exploration. In short, a better understanding of the factors that influence the behavior and decision-making process of those living in and attempting to leave abusive relationships is critical to development of policies and procedures aimed at combating the very serious issue of intimate partner violence.

REFERENCES

[1] Bates, D. S. and Toro, P. A. (1999). Developing measures to assess social support among homeless and poor people. *Journal of Community Psychology* 27(2), 137-156.

[2] Campbell, J. C., Miller, P., Cardwell, M. M. and Belknap, R. A. (1994). Relationship status of battered women over time. *Journal of Family Violence* 9(2), 99-11.

[3] Davis, R. L. (1998). *Domestic violence: Facts and fallacies*. Westport, CT: Praeger.

[4] DeMaris, A. and Swinford, S. (1996). Female victims of spousal violence: Factors influencing their level of fearfulness. *Family Relations* 45(1), 98-106.

[5] DeVoe, E. R. and Smith, E. L. (2003). Don't take my kids: Barriers to service delivery for battered mothers and their young children. *The Journal of Emotional Abuse* 3(3/4), 277-294.

[6] Epstein, D. (1999). In search of effective intervention in domestic violence cases: Rethinking the roles of prosecutors, judges and the court system. *Yale Journal of Law and Feminism* 11(1), 3-50.

[7] Fernandez, M., Iwamoto, K. and Muscat, B. (1997). Dependency and severity of abuse: Impact on women's persistence in utilizing the court

system as protection against domestic violence. *Women and Criminal Justice* 9(1), 39-62.

[8] Frisch, M. B. and MacKenzie, C. J. (1991). A comparison of formerly and chronically battered women on cognitive and situational dimensions. *Psychotherapy* 28, 339-344.

[9] Hathaway, J. E., Mucci, L. A., Silverman, J. G., Brooks, D. R., Matthews, R. and Pavlos, C. A. (2000). Health status and health care use of Massachusetts women reporting partner abuse. *American Journal of Preventive Medicine* 19(4), 302-307.

[10] Herbert, T. B., Silver, R. C. and Ellard, J. H. (1991). Coping with an abusive relationship: How and why do women stay? *Journal of Marriage and the Family* 53(2), 311-325.

[11] Johnson, I. M. (1988). Wife abuse: Factors predictive of the decision-making process of battered women. *Dissertation Abstracts International* 48, 3202A.

[12] Johnson, I. M. (1992). Economic, situational and psychological correlates of the decision-making process of battered women. *Families in Society: The Journal of Contemporary Social Services* 73(3), 168-176.

[13] Kurz, D. (1996). Separation, divorce and woman abuse. *Violence Against Women* 2(1), 63-81.

[14] Langford, D. R. (1996). Predicting unpredictability: A model of women's processes of predicting battering men's violence. *Scholarly Inquiry for Nursing Practice: An International Journal* 10(4), 371-385.

[15] Okun, L. E. (1986). *Woman abuse: facts replacing myths.* Albany: State University of New York Press.

[16] Pape, K. T. and Arias, I. (2000). The role of perceptions and attributions in battered women's intentions to permanently end their violent relationships. *Cognitive Therapy and Research* 24(2), 201-214.

[17] Rhodes, N. R. and McKenzie, E. B. (1998). Why do battered women stay?: Three decades of research. *Aggression and Violent Behavior* 3(4), 391-406.

[18] Roberts, J. C., Wolfer, L. and Mele, M. (2008). Why victims of intimate partner violence withdraw protection orders. *Journal of Family Violence* 23(5), 369-375.

[19] Schutte, N. S., Malouff, J. M. and Doyle, J. S. (1988). The relationship between the characteristics of the victim, persuasive techniques of the batterer and returning to a battered relationship. *Journal of Social Psychology* 128(5), 605-610.

[20] Short, L. M., McMahon, P. M., Chervin, D. D., Shelley, G. A., Lezin, N., Sloop, K. S. and Dawkins, N. (2000). Survivors' identification of protective factors and early warning signs for intimate partner violence. *Violence Against Women* 6(3), 272-285.

[21] Strube, M. J. and Barbour, L. S. (1984). Factors related to the decision to leave an abusive relationship. *Journal of Marriage and the Family* 46(4), 837-844.

[22] Towns, A. and Adams, P. (2000). "If I really loved him enough, he would be okay." *Violence Against Women* 6(6), 558-585.

[23] U.S. Bureau of Census. http://www.census.gov. Accessed on June 1, 2007.

[24] Wilke, D. J. and Vinton, L. (2005). The nature and impact of domestic violence across age cohorts. *Journal of Women and Social Work* 20(3), 316-328.

[25] Wilson, M., Johnson, H. and Daly, M. (1995). Lethal and non-lethal violence against wives. *Canadian Journal of Criminology* 37(3), 331-361.

[26] Zoellner, L. A., Feeny, N. C., Alvarez, J., Watlington, C., O'Neill, M. L., Zager, R. and Foa, E. B. (2000). Factors associated with completion of the restraining order process in female victims of partner violence. *Journal of Interpersonal Violence* 15(10), 1081-1099.

In: New Developments in Human Rights
Editors: J. M. Bauer and C. P. Davies
ISBN 978-1-61324-316-9

Chapter 2

TERRORISM, MIRANDA, AND RELATED MATTERS*

Charles Doyle

ABSTRACT

The Fifth Amendment to the United States Constitution provides in part that "No person ... shall be compelled in any criminal case to be a witness against himself, nor be deprived of life, liberty, or property, without due process of law." In Miranda v. Arizona, the Supreme Court declared that statements of an accused, given during a custodial interrogation, could not be introduced in evidence in criminal proceedings against him, unless he were first advised of his rights and waived them. In Dickerson v. United States, the Court held that the Miranda exclusionary rule was constitutionally grounded and could not be replaced by a statutory provision making all voluntary confessions admissible. In New York v. Quarles, the Court recognized a "limited" "public safety" exception to Miranda, but has not defined the exception further. The lower federal courts have construed the exception narrowly in cases involving unwarned statements concerning the location of a weapon possibly at hand at the time of an arrest.

The Supreme Court has yet to decide to what extent Miranda applies to custodial interrogations conducted overseas. The lower federal courts have held that the failure of foreign law enforcement officials to provide Miranda warnings prior to interrogation does not preclude use of any resulting statement in a subsequent U.S. criminal trial, unless interrogation was a joint

* This is an edited, reformatted and augmented version of CRS Report R41252, dated May 24, 2010..

venture of U.S. and foreign officials or unless the circumstances shock the conscience of the court. They suggest that warnings are a prerequisite for admissibility in U.S. courts following overseas interrogation by U.S. officials.

Miranda applies to courts-martial that are subject to a requirement for an additional warning under the Uniform Code of Military Justice. The statutory provisions governing military commissions call for the admission of some unwarned, involuntary custodial statements. At least one tribunal operating under those provisions has concluded that the Fifth Amendment protections do not apply in the commission trial at Guantanamo Bay of an unprivileged foreign belligerent.

Rule 5 of the Federal Rules of Criminal Procedure requires that federal arrestees be brought before a committing magistrate without unnecessary delay. In the McNabb v. United States and Mallory v. United States cases, the Court declared inadmissible confessions extracted during a period of unnecessary delay. The cases were decided under the Court's supervisory authority over the lower federal courts, and in Corley v. United States, the Court held that McNabb-Mallory had been statutorily supplemented with a provision that made admissible voluntary confession given within six hours of presentment.

Neither *Miranda* nor McNabb-Mallory violations preclude the subsequent prosecution of the accused; they simply preclude the uninvited use of any unwarned, unwaived statements in such prosecutions.

Related legislative proposals have been introduced in the 111th Congress. P.L. 111-84 (H.R. 2647) prohibits members of the military from providing *Miranda* warnings to foreign nationals captured, or held in Defense Department custody, outside the United States as enemy belligerents. Among the legislative proposals yet to secure enactment, one would prohibit the use of funds to provide such warnings (H.R. 2701); others would restrict their use in the interrogation of high- value detainees overseas (S. 3081 and H.R. 4892); and still others would call upon the Administration to provide Congress with information related to the use of *Miranda* warnings in such circumstances (H.R. 3170, H.Res. 537, H.Res. 570, H.Res. 602).

No person ... shall be compelled in any criminal case to be a witness against himself, nor be deprived of life, liberty, or property, without due process of law. U.S. Const. Amend. V.

INTRODUCTION

In *Miranda v. Arizona*, the Supreme Court held that no statement made by an individual during a custodial interrogation may be admitted into evidence against him at his criminal trial, unless he was first warned of his relevant constitutional rights and waived them [1] In New York v. Quarles, the Court later held that the *Miranda* rule was subject to a "public safety" exception [2] Throughout this period, federal law stated that following arrest a suspect should be presented to a magistrate and advised of his rights without "unnecessary delay." [3] Confessions made during the course of any unnecessary delay are generally inadmissible at the suspect's subsequent criminal trial [4]. The realities of contemporary terrorism are such that some have questioned whether these general rules can be, and should be, re-examined and adjusted.

BACKGROUND

Miranda

Before *Miranda*, the Supreme Court relied on the Fifth Amendment in federal cases, but had largely relied upon due process guarantees to exclude a defendant's involuntary confession from his criminal trial in cases that came to it from the states [5] Then, as now, the due process inquiry asks "whether a defendant's will was overborne by the circumstances surrounding the giving of a confession." [6] Recourse to due process was no longer necessary in state cases once it became clear that the Fifth Amendment right was itself binding on the states through the Fourteenth Amendment [7].

In *Miranda*, the Court provided a more specific standard than the "voluntary under the circumstances" due process test. Convinced that the coercive atmosphere of a law enforcement custodial interrogation could undermine the protection against self-incrimination,8 the Court declared that confessions that followed such interrogations could only be admitted in evidence against a defendant if he had been given explicit warnings beforehand.9 That is, the defendant must be warned that he "has the right to remain silent, that anything he says can be used against him in a court of law, that he has the right to the presence of an attorney, and that if he cannot afford an attorney one will be appointed for him prior to any questioning if he so desires." [10]

The warnings having been given, the defendant may explicitly waive them [11] When a defendant requests the presence of an attorney, questioning must stop until one is made available or until the defendant himself initiates the colloquy [12] Authorities may not avoid *Miranda* demands by extracting an unwarned confession, providing the *Miranda* warnings, and then eliciting the same confession, this time "for the record." [13] Nor may authorities persistently return to questioning after an interrogation has been stopped by a defendant's claim of privilege—except upon the arrival of requested defense counsel, at the defendant's invitation, or following a break in interrogation-related custody of at least 14 days [14]

The Court has recognized exceptions to the rule. One, discussed below in greater detail, permits admission into evidence of unwarned statements elicited in the interest of an officer's safety and that of the public [15]. Another permits use of unwarned statements for impeachment purposes [16]. Moreover, on a number of occasions, the Court has declined to recognize a *Miranda* equivalent of the Fourth Amendment's "fruit of the poisonous tree" doctrine [17]

Shortly after *Miranda* was handed down, Congress sought to overturn it by statute, 18 U.S.C. 3501 [18]. For three decades, however, the provision lay dormant, for the Justice Department considered the provision constitutionally suspect, and would not assert it [19]. Thus, when Dickerson v. United States arose in the Fourth Circuit, the Justice Department declined to defend the section's constitutionality [20]. In spite of Justice Department reservations, the Fourth Circuit decided that section "3501, rather than *Miranda*, governs the admissibility of confessions in federal court." [21] The Supreme Court disagreed.22 "*Miranda* announced a constitutional rule," which the Court declined to overrule and which "Congress may not supersede legislatively." [23]

Public Safety Exception

In Quarles, police officers pursued a rape suspect into a supermarket, frisked him, discovered he was wearing an empty holster, and handcuffed him [24]. They asked him where the gun was; he told them, "the gun is over there" (nodding to some empty cartons); they arrested him, and then read him his *Miranda* warnings [25] The Supreme Court recognized that the "case presents a situation where concern for public safety must be paramount to adherence to the literal language of the prophylactic rules enumerated in *Miranda*." [26]

It contrasted the *Miranda* concerns with the exigencies of the case before it. On one hand, "[t]he *Miranda* decision was based in large part on this Court's view that the warnings which it required police to give to suspects in custody would reduce the likelihood that the suspects would fall victim to constitutionally impermissible practices of police interrogation in the presumptively coercive environment of the station house." [27] On the other hand, "[t]he police in this case ... were confronted with the immediate necessity of ascertaining the whereabouts of a gun which they had every reason to believe the suspect had just removed from his empty holster and discarded in the supermarket. So long as the gun was concealed somewhere in the supermarket, with its actual whereabouts unknown, it obviously posed more than one danger to the public safety." [28] The Court perceived the exception as a "narrow" one, and believed police would have no difficulty distinguishing "between questions necessary to secure their own safety or the safety of the public and questions designed solely to elicit testimonial evidence from a suspect." [29]

The Court has yet to further refine the exception, but the lower federal appellate courts have construed it narrowly—some more narrowly than others [30] It has been applied in cases immediately following an arrest when officers have asked an unwarned suspect whether or where a weapon might be found in the immediate area, under circumstances when officers might reasonably believe such a weapon exists and if not secured would pose a danger to themselves or the public [31].

Although the public safety exception, as currently understood, may only be available in limited circumstances in a terrorist context, its existence suggests that the Court might expand its application under compelling circumstances or might recognize other policy-based exceptions to *Miranda* [32].

Miranda Overseas

The Supreme Court has thus far not indicated to what extent, if at all, *Miranda* applies overseas. In fact, it has spoken only infrequently about the extent to which the Fifth Amendment applies outside the United States. Its most recent discussion occurred in Verdugo-Urquidez when it contrasted the difference between the extraterritorial application of the Fourth and Fifth Amendments [33]. There, it noted a violation of the Fifth Amendment privilege against self-incrimination can only occur at trial; a violation of the Fourth Amendment occurs upon the performance of an unreasonable search or seizure—regardless of whether the fruits of the violation are ever offered at trial [34]. For Fifth Amendment purposes, the point of violation is not the place where a statement was coerced, but the place of the criminal proceedings where the statement is offered against the defendant [35]. The Court went on to point out that it previously "rejected the claim that aliens are entitled to Fifth Amendment rights outside the sovereign territory of the United States." [36] Moreover, even where it had recognized that American civilians, subject to U.S. overseas court-martial proceedings, were entitled to some Fifth and Sixth Amendment protections, a majority of the Court had been unwilling to define the precise scope of such entitlement [37].

The lower federal courts, however, have held that the *Miranda* warnings ordinarily do not apply to overseas custodial interrogations conducted by foreign officials. Such unwarned statements may be introduced against the defendant, if voluntary and otherwise admissible.[38] They often identify, but rarely find, two exceptions to this general rule of admissibility—where the interrogation is a joint venture in which U.S. officials are joint participants, or where the circumstances shock the conscience of the court [39].

Implicit in the first exception is that the privilege against self-incrimination—and the attendant *Miranda* requirements—apply to the admissibility in criminal proceedings in this country of statements taken overseas by U.S. law enforcement officers [40] A few courts have suggested that this may be said of the statements of U.S. citizens and foreign nationals alike [41]. They have indicated, however, that "where *Miranda* has been applied to overseas interrogations by U.S. agents, it has been so applied in a flexible fashion to accommodate the exigencies of the local conditions" [42].

In a case in which overseas statements were offered before an overseas tribunal, a military commission tribunal has concluded that the question of the application of the Fifth Amendment extraterritorially requires a case-by-case consideration [43].

Miranda and the Military

As a general rule, *Miranda* applies to custodial interrogations conducted in the course of a military criminal investigation. Both by constitutional imperative and statutory command, unwarned statements are inadmissible against the defendant in any subsequent military prosecution [44].

The statutory provisions applicable to military commissions, however, declare that the Article 83 1(a), (b), and (d) of the Code of Military Justice (10 U.S.C. 83 1(a), (b), and (d), relating to compulsory self-incrimination) shall not apply in commission trials.45 No one may be required to testify against himself in such proceedings [46]. Nor may statements secured by torture or by cruel, inhuman, or degrading treatment be admitted there [47]. Otherwise, statements of the accused may be admitted in evidence, if they are reliable, probative, and either voluntary or were "made incident to lawful conduct during military operations at the point of capture or during closely related active combat engagement, and the interests of justice would best be served by admission of the statement into evidence." [48]

One of the Guantanamo detainees, tried by military commission for the offense of providing material support for terrorism, moved to suppress statements which he contended were secured in violation of the Fifth Amendment [49].

Based on its reading of Boumediene, [50] the tribunal determined that

> when analyzing the extraterritorial application of the Constitution in Guantanamo Bay, the Commission concludes that it should consider (1) the citizenship and status of the detainee and the adequacy of the process through which the status determination was made; (2) the nature of the sites where apprehension and then detention took place; (3) whether practical considerations and exigent circumstances counsel against application of the constitutional right; (4) whether the Executive has provided the accused an adequate substitute for the Constitutional right being sought; (5) whether there is "necessity for the Constitution to apply to prevent injustice; and (6) whether application of the Constitutional right would be "impractical and anomalous." [51]
>
> It further concluded that "[t]he preponderance of these factors analyzed weighs against application of the 5th Amendment in Guantanamo Bay." [52]

McNabb-Mallory

"[T]he rule known simply as McNabb-Mallory generally renders inadmissible confessions made during periods of detention that violate the prompt presentment requirement of Rule 5(a)" [53]. In McNabb v. United States, the Supreme Court was faced with a case in which federal officers had disregarded statutory obligations to promptly present arrested defendants to a committing magistrate [54]. The officers had instead detained and interrogated the suspects over the course of several days, until the confessions upon which the defendants' convictions were based had been extracted.55 The Court found it "unnecessary to reach the Constitutional issues pressed upon" it [56]. Based instead on its supervisory authority over the federal courts, the Court announced that henceforth such confessions, voluntary or involuntary, secured without regard to prompt presentation requirements could not be admitted in evidence against a defendant [57].

When the various statutory presentation requirements were later superseded by rule 5(a) of the Federal Rules of Criminal Procedure (requiring presentation "without unnecessary delay"), no explicit mention was made of either the McNabb exclusionary rule or any other means of enforcement [58] The Court, however, quickly affirmed the continued vitality of McNabb when following the promulgation of rule 5; it reiterated that McNabb applied to both voluntary and involuntary confessions [59] In Mallory, it made clear that any "delay must not be of as a nature to give opportunity for the extraction of confession." [60]

A second provision within section 3501 addresses the McNabb-Mallory rule, 18 U.S.C. 350 1(c). It states that a presentation delay of less than six hours does not by itself render a voluntary confession inadmissible. Recently, the question arose whether, as with *Miranda*, section 3501 was intended to abrogate the McNabb-Mallory, rather than to simply limit its application to voluntary confessions made within six hours of detention [61]. The Court held that Congress intended to modify, not repudiate, McNabb-Mallory [62]. Thus, "[u]nder the rule as revised by §3501(c), a district court with a suppression claim must find whether the defendant confessed within six hours of arrest (unless a longer delay was reasonable considering the means of transportation and the distance to be traveled to the nearest available magistrate)" [63]. If so, the confession is admissible as section 3501(c) provides, "so long as it was made voluntarily and the weight to be given it is left to the jury." [64] If not, "the court must decide whether delaying that long was unreasonable or unnecessary under the McNabb-Mallory cases, and if it was, the confession is to be suppressed" [65].

Legislative Proposals

A number of related legislative proposals have been introduced thus far in the 111th Congress. They include:

P.L. 111-84

Section 1040 of the National Defense Authorization Act for Fiscal Year 2010, P.L. 111-84 (H.R. 2647), 123 Stat. 2454 (2009), prohibits members of the Armed Forces as well as Defense Department officers and employees from providing *Miranda* warnings to foreign nationals captured, or held in Defense Department custody, outside the United States as enemy belligerents. The prohibition does not apply to the Justice Department. The section also directs the Secretary of Defense to report to the Armed Services Committees within 90 days on the impact of providing the warnings to detainees in Afghanistan.

H.R. 2701

Section 504 of the Intelligence Authorization Act for Fiscal Year 2010 (H.R. 2701), as reported out of the House Select Committee on Intelligence (H.Rept. 111-186), would prohibit the use of funds authorized for appropriation under the bill to provide *Miranda* warnings to foreign nationals outside the United States who are either in the custody of the Armed Forces or believed to have terrorist-related information. The House passed H.R. 2701, as amended, on February 26, 2010, 156 Cong. Rec. H946 (daily ed. February 26, 2010).

H.R. 3170

Section 744 of Financial Services and General Government Appropriations Act, 2010 (H.R. 3170), as reported out of the House Appropriations Committee (H.Rept. 111-202), would call upon the Administration to supply Congress with information relating to *Miranda* warnings provided by the Justice Department to foreign nationals who are either in the custody of the Armed Forces or suspected of terrorism. The Consolidated Appropriations Act, 2010, P.L. 111- 117, 123 Stat. 3034 (2009) which absorbed many of the provisions of H.R. 3170, has no comparable provision.

S. 3081

Section 3(b)(3) of the Enemy Belligerent Interrogation, Detention, and Prosecution Act of 2010 (S. 3081), as introduced, would direct that an unprivileged belligerent, interrogated under the bill's procedures relating to high-value detainees, not be given *Miranda* or comparable warnings.

H.R. 4892

Section 3(a)(1)(D) of the Enemy Belligerent Interrogation, Detention, and Prosecution Act of 2010 (H.R. 4892), as introduced, would require the approval of the Director of National Intelligence before *Miranda* warnings could be provided to high-value detainees believed to have terrorism-related information and captured, held, or questioned by an entity with an intelligence community element.

H.Res. 537

H.Res. 537, as adversely reported by the House Judiciary Committee (H.Rept. 111-189), would call upon the Administration to supply Congress with information relating to *Miranda* warnings provided by the Justice Department to foreign nationals who are in the custody of the Armed Forces in Afghanistan and suspected of terrorism.

H.Res. 570

H.Res. 570 would direct the Secretary of Homeland Security to provide the House with information relating to the immigration status of any foreign national captured in Afghanistan who was given *Miranda* warnings by the Justice Department, is in the Defense Department's custody, may be suspected of terrorism, and may be subject to a transfer or release into the United States for civilian or military proceedings.

H.Res. 602

H.Res. 602 would call upon the Administration to provide the House with information, generated on or after January 1, 2005, and relating to the impact of providing *Miranda* warnings to Defense Department detainees in Afghanistan suspected of terrorism.

References

[1] 384 U.S. 436, 468 (1966).

[2] 467 U.S. 649, 655-56 (1984).

[3] F.R.Crim.P. 5(a).

[4] *Mallory v. United States*, 354 U.S. 449, 455 (1957); see also, *McNabb v. United States*, 318 U.S. 332, 345 (1943); *Corley v. United States*, 129 S.Ct. 1558, 1566 (2009); 18 U.S.C. 3501(c).

[5] *Dickerson v. United States*, 530 U.S. 428, 433(2000), citing inter alia *Bram v. United States*, 168 U.S. 532, 542 (1897) and *Brown v. Mississippi*, 297 U.S. 278 (1936), and noting that "Over time, our cases recognized two constitutional bases for the requirement that a confession be voluntary to be admitted into evidence: the Fifth Amendment right against self-incrimination and the Due Process Clause of the Fourteenth Amendment."

[6] *Dickerson v. United States*, 530 U.S. at 434, citing *Schneckloth v. Bustamonte*, 412 U.S. 218, 226 (1973); see also, *Brown v. Mississippi*, 297 U.S. at 287 ("Coercing the supposed state's criminals into confessions and using such confession so coerced from them against them in trials has been the curse of all countries. It was the chief inequity, the crowning infamy of the Star Chamber, and the Inquisition, and other similar institutions. The constitution recognized the evils that lay behind these

practices and prohibited them in this country.... In the instance case, the trial court was fully advised by the undisputed evidence of the way in which the confessions had been procured.... The conviction and sentence were void for want of the essential elements of due process").

[7] *Dickerson v. United States*, 530 U.S. at 434 (parallel citations omitted) ("We have never abandoned this due process jurisprudence, and thus continue to exclude confessions that were obtained involuntarily. But our decisions in *Malloy v. Hogan*, 378 U.S. 1 (1964), and *Miranda* changed the focus of much of the inquiry in determining the admissibility of suspects' incriminating statements. In *Malloy*, we held that the Fifth Amendment's Self-Incrimination Clause is incorporated in the Due Process Clause of the Fourteenth Amendment and thus applies to the States. 378 U.S. at 6-11. We decided *Miranda* on the heels of *Malloy*.").

[8] *Miranda v. Arizona,* 384 U.S. 436, 445-58 (1966).

[9] *Id.* at 467.

[10] *Id.* at 479.

[11] *Id.* at 475.

[12] *Edwards v. Arizona*, 451 U.S. 436, 477-78 (1981).

[13] *Missouri v. Seibert*, 542 U.S. 600, 617 (2004).

[14] *Maryland v. Shatzer*, 130 S.Ct. 1213, 1219-224 (2010).

[15] *New York v. Quarles*, 467 U.S. 649 (1984).

[16] *Harris v. New York*, 401 U.S. 222 (1971).

[17] *United States v. Patane*, 542 U.S. 630, 631-33 (2004); *Oregon v. Elstad*, 470 U.S. 298, 318 (1985); *Michigan v. Tucker*, 417 U.S. 433, 451-52 (1974).

[18] S.Rept. 90-1097, at 51 (1968) ("The committee feels that it is obvious from the opinion of Justice Harlan and other dissenting Justices ... that the overwhelming weight of judicial opinion in this country is that the voluntariness test does not offend the Constitution.... [T]he *Miranda* decision itself was by a bare majority of one, and with increasing frequency the Supreme Court has reversed itself. The committee feels that by the time the issue of constitutionality would reach the Supreme Court, the probability rather is that his legislation would be upheld... .The need for a revision of the *Miranda* decision has been well documented in the proceeding section of this report.").

[19] *Davis v. United States*, 512 U.S. 452, 463-64 (Scalia, J., concurring) ("In fact, with limited exceptions the provision [18 U.S.C. 3501(a)] has been studiously avoided by every Administration, not only in this Court but in the lower courts, since its enactment more than 25 years ago. See Office of Legal Policy, U.S. Dept. of Justice, Report to Attorney General on

Law of Pre-Trial Interrogation 72-73 (1986) (discussing '[t]he abortive implementation of §3501' after its passage in 1968)."); *United States v. Dickerson*, 166 F.3d 667, 682 (4th Cir. 1999) ("The Department of Justice has taken the position that unless the Supreme Court overrules *Miranda*, 'the United States is not free to urge the lower courts' to 'rely on Section 3501.' See Letter from John C. Keeney, Acting Assistant Attorney General, to all United States Attorneys and all Criminal Division Section Chiefs (Nov. 6, 1997).").

[20] *Id.* at 680-82.

[21] *Id.* at 692.

[22] *Dickerson v. United States*, 530 U.S. 428, 438 (2000).

[23] *Id.* at 444.

[24] 467 U.S. 649, 651-52 (1984).

[25] *Id.* at 652.

[26] *Id.* at 653.

[27] *id.* at 656.

[28] *Id.* at 657.

[29] *Id.*

[30] *Matters of Public Safety and the Current Quarrel Over the Scope of the* Quarles *Exception to* Miranda, 78 FORDHAM LAW REVIEW 1931, 1931 (2010) ("However, latent ambiguity arising from the *Quarles* decision authored by [then] Justice William Rehnquist has resulted in a split among the federal courts of appeals as to what constitutes a 'public safety threat.' Some courts broadly extend the Quarles exception to inherently dangerous situations, including the threat of an officer mishandling an undiscovered weapon. Other courts narrowly apply *Quarles* to exigent circumstances where there is actual evidence that a suspect or other third party could inflict immediate harm to officers or the public.").

[31] *United States v. Are*, 590 F.3d 499, 506 (7th Cir. 2009) ("We, too, have concluded that questioning a suspect about whether he has a gun may fall within *Quarles*' public safety exception.... The FBI agent's question to Daniels about the presence of a weapon in the house falls within the public safety exception to Miranda. The question seemed reasonably prompted by a concern for the public safety. Though Daniels was cuffed and the officers and agents had conducted a brief protective sweep, they knew ... he had several prior drug and weapons offenses. But they did not know the location of any weapon that he may have had in the house. A weapon might have been hidden near the place where the officers placed Daniels before taking him outside and thus would have been within his reach.... Furthermore, the

presence of Daniels' wife and children bolsters the conclusion that the question about the weapon falls within the public safety exception."); *United States v. Jackson*, 544 F.3d 351, 360 n.9 (1st Cir. 2008) ("The government also argues that the statements at the apartment are admissible, even if they were the product of custodial interrogation, under the public safety exception to *Miranda*'s suppression requirement. The government's contention is without merit. The gun, stuffed inside a cereal box in the refrigerator, was clearly outside of the reach of Jackson, who was not even in the apartment and, in any event, was surrounded by a number of police officers."); *United States v. Liddell*, 517 F.3d 1007, 1011-12 (8th Cir. 2008) ("As I read *Quarles*, the public safety exception to *Miranda* applies only when (1) an immediate danger to the police officers or the public exists, or (2) when the public may later come upon a weapon and thereby create an immediately dangerous situation."); *United States v. Williams*, 483 F.3d 425, 429 (6th Cir. 2007) ("An officer may rely on the public safety exception only if he has a[n] objectively reasonable belief that he is in danger."); *United States v. DeJear*, 552 F.3d 1196, 1201 (10th 2009) (citing *Williams* with approval); see also *United States v. Spoerke*, 568 F.3d 1236, 1249 (11th Cir. 2009); *United States v. Jones*, 567 F.3d 712, 714-17 (D.C.Cir. 2009); *United States v. Reyes*, 353 F.3d 148, 152-55 (2d Cir. 2003).

[32] Cf., *In re Terrorist Bombings of U.S. Embassies in East Africa*, 552 F.3d 177, 203 (2d Cir. 2008)("*Miranda*'s public safety exception would likely apply overseas with no less force than it does domestically. When exigent circumstances compel an un-warned interrogation in order to protect the public, Miranda would not impair the government's ability to obtain that information. Second, we emphasize that the Miranda framework governs only the admission of custodial statements at U.S. trials. In so far as U.S. agents do not seek to introduce statements obtained through overseas custodial interrogations at U.S. trials").

[33] *United States v. Verdugo-Urquidez*, 494 U.S. 259, 264-74 (1990).

[34] *Id.* at 264.

[35] *Id.* ("The privilege against self-incrimination guaranteed by the Fifth Amendment is a fundamental trial right to criminal defendants. Although conduct by law enforcement officials prior to trial may ultimately impair that right, a constitutional violation occurs only at trial.")

[36] *Id.* at 269, citing *Johnson v. Eisentrager*, 339 U.S. 763 (1950).

[37] *Id.* at 269-70, citing *Reid v. Covert*, 354 U.S. 1, 75 (1957) (Harlan, J., concurring in the result).

[38] *United States v. Frank*, 599 F.3d 1221, 1228 (1 1th Cir. 2010); *United States v. Abu Ali*, 528 F.3d 210, 227 (4th Cir. 2008); *United States v. Yousef*, 327 F.3d 56, 145 (2d Cir. 2003); *United States v. Heller*, 625 F.2d 594, 599 (5th Cir. 1980); *United States v. Mundt*, 508 F.2d 904, 906 (10th Cir. 1974); *United States v. Chavarria*, 443 F.2d 904, 905 (9th Cir. 1971); *United States v. Mendes-Mesquita*, 541 F.Supp.2d 30, 34 (D.D.C. 2008); *United States v. Marzook*, 435 F.Supp.2d 708, 743 (N.D. Ill. 2006); *United States v. Ravine*, 11 M.J. 325, 329 (C.M.A. 1981).

[39] *United States v. Frank*, 599 F.3d at 1228-229; *United States v. Abu Ali*, 528 F.3d at 227-28; *United States v. Yousef*, 327 F.3d at 145-46; *United States v. Heller*, 625 F.2d at 599; *United States v. Mundt*, 508 F.2d at 906-907; *United States v. Karake*, 443 F.Supp.2d 8, 49 (D.D.C. 2006); *United States v. Marzook*, 435 F.Supp.2d at 743-44; *United States v. Jones*, 6 M.J. 226, 229 (C.M.A. 1979).

[40] Cf., *In re Terrorist Bombings*, 552 F.3d 177, 203 (2d Cir. 2008) ("Other circuits have explicitly recognized the applicability of *Miranda* to custodial statements elicited overseas through the active participation of U.S. agents. In light of these precedents, we are proceeding on the assumption that the *Miranda* 'warning/waiver' framework generally governs the admissibility in our domestic courts of custodial statements obtained by U.S. officials from individuals during their detention under the authority of foreign governments."), citing *United States v. Heller*, 625 F.2d 594, 599 (5th Cir. 1980) and *Pfeifer v. U.S. Bureau of Prisons*, 615 F.2d 873, 877 (9th Cir. 1980).

[41] *United States v. Clarke*, 611 F.Supp.2d 12, 29-30 (D.D.C. 2009) ("It is by now well-established that the Fifth Amendment privilege against self-incrimination protects nonresident aliens facing a criminal trial in the United States even where the questioning by United States authorities takes place abroad."), citing *In re Terrorist Bombings*, 552 F.3d at 198-201; *United States v. Yousef*, 327 F.3d at 145-46; *United States v. Straker*, 596 F.Supp.2d 80, 90 (D.D.C. 2009).

[42] *United States v. Clarke*, 611 F.Supp.2d at 30 (D.D.C. 2009), citing *In re Terrorist Bombings*, 552 F.3d at 204-205; *United States v. Dopf*, 434 F.2d 205, 207 (5th Cir. 1970); *Cranford v. Rodriguez*, 512 F.2d 860, 862-63 (10th Cir. 1975).

[43] United States v. Hamdan, 1 M.C.Rept. 121 (M.C. 2008), available at http://www.wcl.american.edu/nimj/ military _commission.cfm.

[44] *United States v. Tempia*, 16 C.M.A. 629, 635-37 (1967); *United States v. DeLaRosa*, 67 M.J. 318, 320 (C.A.A.F. 2009) ("Prior to initiating

interrogation, law enforcement officials must provide rights warnings to a person in custody. Military officials and civilians acting on their behalf are required to provide rights warnings prior to interrogating a member of the armed forces if that service member is a suspect, irrespective of custody."), citing *Miranda v. Arizona,* 384 U.S. 436, 445 (1966); *United States v. Tempia*, 16 C.M.A. 629, 637 (1967); U.S. Const. Amend. V; Article 31(b), USMJ (10 U.S.C. 831(b)), and Military Rules of Evidence 305(b)(1), 305(c).

[45] 10 U.S.C. 948b(d)(1)(B).

[46] 10 U.S.C. 948(b).

[47] 10 U.S.C. 948r(a) ("except against a person accused of torture or such treatment as evidence that the statement was made").

[48] 10 U.S.C. 948r(c), (d).

[49] *United States v. Hamdan*, 1 M.C.Rept. at 121. Hamdan sought to enjoin his trial by military commission. Without going to the merits, the court refused the injunction, but noted with regard to an earlier version of the admissibility of involuntary statements: "Another departure [from the standards that would apply in either U.S. criminal trials or courts- martial], and a startling one, is that under 10 U.S.C. §948r(c), evidence obtained by 'coercion' may be used against the defendant so long as the military judge decides that its admission is in the interest of justice and that it has 'sufficient' probative value. *Compare Chambers v. Florida*, 309 U.S. 227 (1940) (reversing conviction and excluding evidence obtained through five days of coercive interrogation)," *Hamdan v. Gates*, 565 F.Supp.2d 130, 132 (D.D.C. 2008).

[50] *Boumediene v. Bush*, 128 S.Ct. 2229 (2008).

[51] *United States v. Hamdan*, 1 M.C.Rept. at 131.

[52] *Id.* at 134. A second military commission tribunal appears to have concluded as well that suppression issues should be resolved under commission rules—instructed, but not governed, by Fifth Amendment principles, *United States v. Jaward*, 1 M.C.Rept. 349, 350 n.5 (M.C. 2008) ("The Supreme Court's opinion in *Elstad* was based, in part, on the Fifth Amendment self-incrimination and warning requirements that were put in place in *Miranda v. Arizona*, 451 U.S. 471 (1966) as a practical reinforcement of those rights. While, in the case at bar, the accused's self-incrimination protections are set forth in M.C.R.E. 301 and M.C.R.E. 304, a reasonably similar *Elsad* analysis is appropriate with regard to the admissibility of confessions allegedly the product of coercion.").

[53] *Corley v. United States*, 129 S.Ct. 1558, 1563 (2009).

[54] 318 U.S. 332, 342-44 (1943), citing 18 U.S.C. 595, 593; and 5 U.S.C. 300a (1940 ed.).

[55] *Id.* at 334-38.

[56] *Id.* at 340.

[57] *Id.* at 349.

[58] F.R.Crim.P. 5(a), 18 U.S.C. App. (1946 ed.).

[59] *Upshaw v. United States*, 335 U.S. 410, 412 (1948).

[60] *Mallory v. United States*, 354 U.S. 449, 455 (1957); see also *Corley v. United States*, 129 S.Ct. 1558, 1563 (2009) ("delay for the purpose of interrogation is the epitome of 'unnecessary delay'"); *County of Riverside v. McLaughlin*, 500 U.S. 44, 61 (1991) (Scalia, J., dissenting) ("the only element bearing upon the reasonableness of delay was not such circumstances as the pressing need to conduct further investigation, but the arresting officer's ability, once the prisoner had been secured, to reach a magistrate.").

[61] *Corley v. United States*, 129 S.Ct. 1558 (2009).

[62] at 1571.

[63] *Id.*

[64] *Id.*

[65] *Id.*

In: New Developments in Human Rights
Editors: J. M. Bauer and C. P. Davies

ISBN 978-1-61324-316-9

Chapter 3

JUDICIAL ACTIVITY CONCERNING ENEMY COMBATANT DETAINEES: MAJOR COURT RULINGS

Jennifer K. Elsea[*] *and Michael John Garcia*

SUMMARY

As part of the conflict with Al Qaeda and the Taliban, the United States has captured and detained numerous persons believed to have been part of or associated with enemy forces. Over the years, federal courts have considered a multitude of petitions by or on behalf of suspected belligerents challenging aspects of U.S. detention policy. Although the Supreme Court has issued definitive rulings concerning several legal issues raised in the conflict with Al Qaeda and the Taliban, many others remain unresolved, with some the subject of ongoing litigation.

This report discusses major judicial opinions concerning suspected enemy belligerents detained in the conflict with Al Qaeda and the Taliban. The report addresses all Supreme Court decisions concerning enemy combatants. It also discusses notable circuit court opinions addressing issues of ongoing relevance to U.S. detention policy. The report also addresses a few notable decisions by federal district courts that are the subject of ongoing *habeas* litigation. Finally, it describes a few federal court rulings in criminal cases involving persons who were

[*] Email: jelsea@crs.loc.gov

either involved in the 9/11 attacks or were captured abroad by U.S. forces during operations against Al Qaeda, the Taliban, and associated entities.

Many of the rulings discussed in this report are discussed in greater detail in other CRS products, including CRS Report RL33180, *Enemy Combatant Detainees: Habeas Corpus Challenges in Federal Court*, by Jennifer K. Elsea and Michael John Garcia; CRS Report RL34536, *Boumediene v. Bush: Guantanamo Detainees' Right to Habeas Corpus*, by Michael John Garcia; and CRS Report RS2 1884, *The Supreme Court 2003 Term: Summary and Analysis of Opinions Related to Detainees in the War on Terrorism*, by Jennifer K. Elsea.

As part of the conflict with the Taliban and Al Qaeda, the United States has captured and detained numerous persons believed to have been part of or associated with enemy forces. Over the years, federal courts have considered a multitude of petitions by or on behalf of suspected belligerents challenging aspects of U.S. detention policy. The Supreme Court has issued definitive rulings concerning several legal issues raised in the conflict with Al Qaeda and the Taliban, including executive authority under the 2001 Authorization to Use Military Force (AUMF; P.L. 107-40) to detain properly-designated enemy belligerents captured on the Afghan battlefield; the application of at least some provisions of the 1949 Geneva Conventions to the conflict with Al Qaeda; and the ability of detainees held in the United States or at the U.S. Naval Station in Guantanamo Bay, Cuba to challenge the legality of their detention in *habeas corpus* proceedings. However, many other issues remain the subject of ongoing litigation, including the full scope of the Executive's detention authority; the degree to which noncitizens held at Guantanamo and other locations outside the United States are entitled to protections under the Constitution; and the authority of federal *habeas* courts to compel the release of such detainees into the United States if the Executive cannot effectuate their release to another country.

This report briefly summarizes major judicial opinions concerning suspected enemy belligerents[1] detained in the conflict with Al Qaeda and the Taliban. It discusses all Supreme Court decisions concerning enemy combatants. It also

---

[1] The Obama Administration has discontinued the use of the term "enemy combatant" to describe persons detained pursuant to the law of war or the Authorization to Use Military Force (AUMF). *See* Department of Justice (DOJ), "Department of Justice Withdraws 'Enemy Combatant' Definition for Guantanamo Detainees," press release, March 13, 2009, http://www.usdoj.gov/opa/pr/2009/March/09-ag-232.html (hereinafter "DOJ Press Release"); In re Guantanamo Bay Detainee Litigation, Respondents' Memorandum Regarding the Government's Detention Authority Relative to Detainees Held At Guantanamo Bay, No. 08-0442, filed March 13, 2009 (D.D.C.) (hereinafter "Detention Authority Memorandum"). We use the terms "enemy combatant" or "enemy belligerent" broadly to describe persons who might be subject to detention or prosecution in connection with the conflict authorized by the AUMF as interpreted by the executive branch.

addresses notable circuit court opinions addressing issues of ongoing relevance to U.S. detention policy. The report also discusses a few notable decisions by federal district courts that are the subject of ongoing *habeas* litigation. Finally, it addresses selected federal court rulings in criminal cases involving persons who were either involved in the 9/11 attacks or were captured abroad by U.S. forces during operations against Al Qaeda and the Taliban.

Many of the rulings discussed in this report are discussed in greater detail in other CRS products, including CRS Report RL33180, *Enemy Combatant Detainees: Habeas Corpus Challenges in Federal Court*, by Jennifer K. Elsea and Michael John Garcia; CRS Report RL34536, *Boumediene v. Bush: Guantanamo Detainees' Right to Habeas Corpus*, by Michael John Garcia; and CRS Report RS2 1884, *The Supreme Court 2003 Term: Summary and Analysis of Opinions Related to Detainees in the War on Terrorism*, by Jennifer K. Elsea.

SUPREME COURT DECISIONS

Since 2004, the Supreme Court has made several rulings concerning enemy combatants. These have addressed, *inter alia*, the Executive's authority to detain enemy belligerents under the 2001 AUMF; the legality of military commissions established by presidential order to try suspected belligerents for violations of the law of war; and detainees' access to federal courts.

Hamdi v. Rumsfeld, 542 U.S. 507 (2004)[2]

The *Hamdi* case addressed the President's authority to detain "enemy combatants" as part of the conflict authorized by the AUMF, and whether a detained individual could seek independent review of the legality of his detention. Four separate opinions were written, with none receiving support of a majority of the justices. However, a majority of the Court recognized that, as a necessary incident to the 2001 AUMF, the President is authorized to detain persons captured while fighting U.S. forces in Afghanistan (including U.S. citizens), and potentially hold such persons for the duration of the conflict to prevent their return to hostilities.[3] A

---

[2] For further discussion of *Hamdi*, see CRS Report RS2 1884, *The Supreme Court 2003 Term: Summary and Analysis of Opinions Related to Detainees in the War on Terrorism*, by Jennifer K. Elsea.

[3] Hamdi v. Rumsfeld, 542 U.S. 507, 518 (2004) (O'Connor, J., plurality opinion); *id.* at 588-589 (Thomas, J., dissenting).

divided Court found that persons deemed "enemy combatants" have the right to challenge the legality of their detention before a judge or other "neutral decision-maker," with a majority clearly recognizing the existence of such a right in the case of a detained U.S. citizen.[4] In a plurality opinion joined by three other Justices, Justice O'Connor wrote that a citizen detained as an enemy combatant must receive notice of the factual basis for his classification and a fair opportunity to rebut the government's factual assertions before a neutral decision-maker, and has a right to counsel in connection with such a hearing. The plurality, suggested, however, that the exigencies of the circumstances of a detainee's capture may allow for a tailoring of enemy combatant proceedings "to alleviate their uncommon potential to burden the Executive at a time of ongoing military conflict," possibly allowing hearsay evidence and "a presumption in favor of the Government's evidence," as long as a fair opportunity to rebut such evidence is provided.[5]

Rumsfeld v. Padilla, 542 U.S. 426 (2004)[6]

The *Padilla* case, decided on the same day as *Hamdi*, concerned a *habeas* challenge by Jose Padilla, a U.S. citizen being held on U.S. soil as an "enemy combatant." Unlike Hamdi, however, Padilla was captured on U.S. soil, where he was declared an "enemy combatant" and militarily detained for his alleged involvement in an Al Qaeda plot to detonate a "dirty bomb." In a 5-4 ruling, the Court remanded the case without deciding the merits on the ground that Padilla's *habeas* petition had not been filed in the proper venue. In doing so, the majority did not reach the merits of Padilla's claim that any authority the President might have under the AUMF to detain "enemy combatants" did not extend to persons captured on American soil and away from the Afghan battlefield. Four Justices would have found jurisdiction based on the "exceptional circumstances" of the case and affirmed the holding below that detention is prohibited under the Non-Detention Act, 18 U.S.C. § 4001(a) (prohibiting the detention of U.S. citizens

---

[4] *Id.* at 518, 533 (O'Connor, J., plurality opinion, joined by Breyer, J., Kennedy, J., and Rehnquist, C.J.); 553 (Souter, J., concurring in part and dissenting in part, joined by Ginsburg, J.). Justices Scalia and Stevens supported a more limited view concerning the Executive's authority to detain U.S. citizens, believing that detention without criminal charge was only permissible if Congress suspended the writ of *habeas corpus*. *Id.* at 554 (Scalia, J., dissenting, joined by Stevens, J.).

[5] *Id.* at 533-534 (O'Connor, J., plurality opinion).

[6] For further discussion of the *Padilla* decision, see CRS Report RS21884, *The Supreme Court 2003 Term: Summary and Analysis of Opinions Related to Detainees in the War on Terrorism*, by Jennifer K. Elsea, *supra* footnote 2.

unless authorized by an act of Congress). Padilla filed a new petition in the Fourth Circuit, and the appellate court considered the legality of his detention in *Padilla v. Haft*, discussed *infra*.

Rasul v. Bush, 542 U.S. 466 (2004)[7]

In *Rasul v. Bush*, the Court held in a 6-3 ruling that the federal *habeas corpus* statute, 28 U.S.C. § 2241, provided federal courts with jurisdiction to consider *habeas corpus* petitions by or on behalf of persons detained at the U.S. Naval Station in Guantanamo Bay, Cuba. Having found that Guantanamo detainees were entitled by statute to seek *habeas* review of their detention, the Court did not reach the issue of whether the constitutional writ of *habeas* also extended to noncitizens held at Guantanamo. Congress subsequently attempted to limit the reach of the federal *habeas* statute to Guantanamo detainees through the enactment of the Detainee Treatment Act of 2005 (DTA)[8] and the Military Commissions Act of 2006 (MCA).[9]

Hamdan v. Rumsfeld, 548 U.S. 557 (2006)[10]

In *Hamdan v. Rumsfeld*, the Supreme Court reviewed the validity of military tribunals established pursuant to presidential order to try suspected terrorists for violations of the law of war. The petitioner Hamdan was charged with conspiracy to commit a violation of the law of war. Prior to reaching the merits of the case, the *Hamdan* Court first had to determine whether the DTA stripped it of jurisdiction to review *habeas corpus* challenges by or on behalf of Guantanamo detainees whose petitions had already been filed prior to enactment of the DTA. In a 5-3 opinion, the Court held that the DTA did not apply to such petitions. Turning to the merits of the case, the majority held that the convened tribunals did not comply with the Uniform Code of Military Justice (UCMJ) or the law of war, as incorporated in the UCMJ and embodied in 1949 Geneva Conventions, which the Court held applicable to the armed conflict with Al Qaeda. The Court held that, at a minimum, Common Article 3 of the Geneva Conventions applies to

[7] For a more detailed summary of the *Rasul* opinion, see *id.*

[8] P.L. 109-148, Title X; P.L. 109-163, Title XIV.

[9] P.L. 109-366.

[10] For further discussion of the *Hamdan* opinion, see CRS Report RS22466, *Hamdan v. Rumsfeld: Military Commissions in the "Global War on Terrorism,"* by Jennifer K. Elsea.

persons captured in the conflict with Al Qaeda, according to them a minimum baseline of protections, including protection from the "passing of sentences and the carrying out of executions without previous judgment pronounced by a regularly constituted court, affording all the judicial guarantees which are recognized as indispensable by civilized peoples." The Court held that military commissions were not "regularly constituted" because they deviated too far from the rules that apply to courts-martial, without a satisfactory explanation of the need for departing from such rules. In particular, the Court noted that the commission rules allowing the exclusion of the defendant from attending portions of his trial or hearing some of the evidence against him deviated substantially from court-martial procedures.

A four-justice plurality of the Court also recognized that for an act to be triable under the common law of war, the precedent for it being treated as an offense must be "plain and unambiguous."[11] After examining the history of military commission practice in the United States and internationally, the plurality further concluded that conspiracy to violate the law of war was not in itself a crime under the common law of war or the UCMJ.

Boumediene v. Bush, 553 U.S.__, 128 S.Ct. 2229 (2008)[12]

In the aftermath of the *Hamdan* decision, Congress enacted the Military Commissions Act of 2006 (MCA), which, *inter alia*, expressly eliminated court jurisdiction over all pending and future causes of action other than the limited review permitted under the DTA. In the 2008 case of *Boumediene v. Bush*, the Court ruled in a 5-4 opinion that the constitutional privilege of *habeas* extends to Guantanamo detainees.[13] In doing so, the Court stated that the Constitution's extraterritorial application turns on "objective factors and practical concerns."[14] The Court deemed at least three factors to be relevant in assessing the extraterritorial scope of the constitutional writ of *habeas*: (1) the citizenship and status of the detainee and the adequacy of the status determination process; (2) the nature of the site where the person is seized and detained; and (3) practical obstacles inherent in resolving the prisoner's entitlement to the writ.

---

[11] Hamdan v. Rumsfeld, 548 U.S. 557, 602 (2006) (Stevens, J., plurality opinion, joined by Souter, J., Ginsburg, J., and Breyer, J.).

[12] A more extensive discussion of *Boumediene* is found in CRS Report RL34536, *Boumediene v. Bush: Guantanamo Detainees' Right to Habeas Corpus*, by Michael John Garcia.

[13] Boumediene v. Bush, 553 U.S. __, 128 S.Ct. 2229 (2008).

[14] *Id.* at 2258.

The Court also found that MCA § 7, which limited judicial review of executive determinations of the *Boumediene* petitioners' enemy combatant status to that authorized by the DTA, did not provide an adequate *habeas* substitute and therefore acted as an unconstitutional suspension of the writ of *habeas corpus*. The majority listed a number of potential constitutional infirmities in the DTA review process, including the absence of provisions (1) empowering a reviewing court to order the release of a detainee found to be unlawfully held; (2) permitting petitioners to challenge the President's authority to detain them indefinitely; (3) enabling a presiding court to review or correct administrative findings of fact which formed the legal basis for an individual's detention; and (4) permitting the detainee to present exculpatory evidence discovered after the conclusion of administrative proceedings.

Although the *Boumediene* Court held that the constitutional writ of *habeas* extends to noncitizens held at Guantanamo, it did not opine as to the scope of *habeas* review available to detainees, the remedy available for those persons found to be unlawfully held by the United States, and the extent to which other constitutional provisions extend to noncitizens held at Guantanamo and elsewhere.

Gates v. Bismullah, 128 S.Ct. 2960 (2008) (Mem.)

Prior to the Supreme Court's decision in *Boumediene*, the D.C. Circuit Court of Appeals considered a number of challenges brought under the DTA in which detainees contested determinations by Combatant Status Review Tribunals (CSRTs) that they were properly detained as enemy combatants. In 2008, the government petitioned the Supreme Court to review two rulings by the D.C. Circuit regarding the scope of judicial review of CSRT determinations.[15] The Supreme Court granted certiorari and vacated the appellate court's decisions, remanding for reconsideration in light of the Supreme Court's decision in *Boumediene*. Upon remand, the D.C. Circuit reinstated without explanation its

---

[15] The D.C. Circuit in July 2007 issued an order rejecting the government's motion to limit the scope of the court's review to the official record of the CSRT hearings. Bismullah v. Gates, 501 F.3d 178 (*Bismullah I*). The circuit court decided that in order to determine whether a preponderance of evidence supported the CSRT determinations, it must have access to all the information a CSRT is "authorized to obtain and consider, pursuant to the procedures specified by the Secretary of Defense." The court thereafter denied the government's request for rehearing, explaining its view that its previous order would not require a search for information that was not "reasonably available." Bismullah v. Gates, 503 F.3d 137(D.C. Cir. 2007) (*Bismullah II*).

decisions, presumably because it did not find the *Boumediene* ruling to conflict with its decisions in these cases.

al-Marri v. Spagone, 129 S.Ct. 1545 (2009)

In December 2008, the Supreme Court granted certiorari to review an *en banc* ruling by the Fourth Circuit Court of Appeals regarding petitioner al-Marri, a lawful alien resident who had been arrested in the United States and thereafter detained as an enemy combatant. At the time, the Court's decision to review the Fourth Circuit's ruling was thought to have potentially set the stage for a definitive pronouncement regarding the President's authority to militarily detain terrorist suspects apprehended away from the Afghan battlefield. However, before the Court could consider the merits of the case, the government requested that the Court authorize al-Marri's release from military custody and transfer to civilian authorities to face criminal charges. The Court granted the government's request, vacated the appellate court's earlier judgment, and transferred the case back to the lower court with orders to dismiss it as moot. (See below for discussion of appellate court ruling).

Kiyemba v. Obama, 130 S.Ct. 1235 (2010)

In October 2009, the Supreme Court agreed to review a ruling by a three-judge panel of the D.C. Circuit Court of Appeals in the case of *Kiyemba v. Obama*, discussed *infra*. The *Kiyemba* case involved several Guantanamo detainees who, despite no longer being considered enemy combatants and been cleared for release, had not been transferred from Guantanamo on account of the government being unable to effectuate their release to a foreign country. The *Kiyemba* petitioners sought reversal of a D.C. Circuit ruling finding that a federal habeas court lacked the authority to compel the Executive to release the detainees into the United States. Following the Supreme Court's grant of certiorari, however, several *Kiyemba* petitioners were resettled in foreign countries, and the United States was able to find countries willing to settle the remaining petitioners, although five petitioners rejected these countries' offers for resettlement. On March 1, 2010, the Supreme Court vacated the appellate court's opinion and remanded the case in light of these developments. Because the Supreme Court had granted certiorari on the understanding that no remedy was available for the petitioners other than release into the United States, it returned the case to the

D.C. Circuit to review the ramifications of the new circumstances. Litigation in *Kiyemba* remains ongoing.

NOTABLE CIRCUIT COURT RULINGS

The following section discusses major rulings made at the appellate court level regarding persons designated as enemy combatants that involve matters of continuing relevance to U.S. detention policy. It does not discuss those rulings that were subsequently overruled by the Supreme Court on the merits.

Padilla v. Hanft, 423 F.3d 386 (4th Cir. 2005)

After the Supreme Court vacated a ruling in his favor by the Second Circuit (see above), Jose Padilla filed a new petition in the District Court for the District of South Carolina. The district court granted Padilla's motion for summary judgment and ordered the government to release him from military detention, while suggesting Padilla could be kept in civilian custody if charged with a crime or determined to be a material witness.[16] Padilla's attorneys had based their argument on the dissenting opinion of four Supreme Court Justices, who would have found Padilla's detention barred by the Non-Detention Act, 18 U.S.C. § 400 1(a), and the language in *Hamdi* seemingly limiting the scope of detention authority under the AUMF to combatants captured in Afghanistan. The government argued that Padilla's detention is covered under the *Hamdi* decision's interpretation of the AUMF as an act of Congress authorizing his detention because he is alleged to have attended an Al Qaeda training camp in Afghanistan before traveling to Pakistan and then to the United States.[17] The judge disagreed with the government, finding that more express authority from Congress would be necessary and that the AUMF contains no such authority. Accordingly, the court found Padilla's detention barred by 18 U.S.C. § 400 1(a). The court also disagreed that the President has inherent authority as Commander-in-Chief of the Armed Forces to determine wartime measures.[18]

The Fourth Circuit Court of Appeals reversed, finding that Padilla, although captured in the United States, could be detained pursuant to the AUMF because he

[16] Padilla v. Hanft, 389 F. Supp. 2d 678 (D.S.C. 2005).

[17] *See* Respondents' Answer to the Petition for a Writ of Habeas Corpus at 2, Padilla v. Hanft, C/A No. 02:04 222 1- 26AJ (D.S.C. filed 2004).

[18] 389 F. Supp. 2d at 690.

had been, prior to returning to the United States, "'armed and present in a combat zone' in Afghanistan as part of Taliban forces during the conflict there with the United States."[19] As the Supreme Court again considered whether to grant review, the government charged Padilla with conspiracy based on evidence unrelated to the original "dirty bomb" plot allegations and petitioned for leave to transfer him from military custody to a federal prison for civilian trial.[20] The Court granted the government permission to transfer Padilla[21] and later denied certiorari.[22] Padilla was found guilty and sentenced to 17 years and three months' imprisonment, the trial court having rejected his motion to dismiss charges against him due to his alleged mistreatment at the hands of the military.[23]

al-Marri v. Pucciarelli, 534 F.3d 213 (2008) (per curiam)[24]

In *al-Marri*, the Fourth Circuit sitting *en banc* considered whether the AUMF and the law of war permit the detention of a resident alien alleged to have engaged in activities within the United States in support of Al Qaeda, but who had not been part of the conflict in Afghanistan. Four of the nine judges would have held that even if the allegations were true, al-Marri did not fit within the legal category

---

[19] 423 F.3d 386, 390-91 (4th Cir. 2005).

[20] The government initially asked the Fourth Circuit to approve Padilla's transfer and suggested it should vacate its opinion, but the judges preferred to defer to the Supreme Court to make that determination. In rejecting the government's application, Circuit Judge Luttig (who has since stepped down from the bench) issued a harsh opinion expressing disappointment at the government's decision abruptly to abandon its position that national security imperatives demanded Padilla's continued military detention:

> [A]s the government surely must understand, although the various facts it has asserted are not necessarily inconsistent or without basis, its actions have left not only the impression that Padilla may have been held for these years, even if justifiably, by mistake—an impression we would have thought the government could ill afford to leave extant. They have left the impression that the government may even have come to the belief that the principle in reliance upon which it has detained Padilla for this time, that the President possesses the authority to detain enemy combatants who enter into this country for the purpose of attacking America and its citizens from within, can, in the end, yield to expediency with little or no cost to its conduct of the war against terror—an impression we would have thought the government likewise could ill afford to leave extant.

Padilla v. Hanft, 432 F.3d 582, 587 (4th Cir. 2005)(order).

[21] Padilla v. Hanft, 546 U.S. 1084 (2006).

[22] 547 U.S. 1062 (2006).

[23] United States v. Padilla, 2007 WL 1079090 (S.D.Fla. 2007) (unreported opinion). However, another district court held Padilla can pursue civil damages against a former government official for his treatment in military detention. Padilla v. Yoo, 633 F. Supp. 2d 1005 (N.D.Cal. 2009).

[24] For further discussion of *al-Marri*, see CRS Report RL33 180, *Enemy Combatant Detainees: Habeas Corpus Challenges in Federal Court*, by Jennifer K. Elsea and Michael John Garcia.

of "enemy combatant" within the meaning of *Hamdi*, and that the government could continue to hold him only if it charged him with a crime, commenced deportation proceedings, or obtained a material witness warrant in connection with grand jury proceedings (as a majority of the original three-judge panel had found). A plurality of the fractured *en banc* court, however, found that the AUMF and the law of war give the President the power to detain persons who enter the United States as "sleeper agents" on behalf of Al Qaeda for the purpose of committing hostile and war-like acts such as those carried out on 9/11 (although the judges did not arrive at a common definition of "enemy combatant"). The case was remanded to the district court for further consideration of the evidence to determine whether the government had established that al-Marri was a sleeper agent.

The *en banc* panel also considered the evidentiary burden that the government would be required to fulfill to detain al-Marri as an enemy combatant. In his controlling opinion, Judge Traxler wrote that the lower court had erred in applying the relaxed evidentiary standards of *Hamdi* to persons captured in the United States. While the *Hamdi* plurality suggested that hearsay evidence might be sufficient to support detention of a person apprehended in combat zone, Judge Traxler wrote that *Hamdi* does not establish a "cookie-cutter procedure appropriate for every alleged enemy-combatant, regardless of the circumstances of the alleged combatant's seizure or the actual burdens the government might face in defending the *habeas* petition in the normal way."[25] However, he recognized that some relaxation of normal procedural safeguards may be warranted if the government demonstrates the need for this relaxation on account of national security interests and an undue burden that would result if it was compelled to produce more reliable evidence. After the Supreme Court granted review, the government brought charges against al-Marri in federal court and asked the Court to dismiss the case as moot and to vacate the decision below, which the Court agreed to do, leaving the applicability of the AUMF to persons captured in the United States uncertain. Al-Marri pleaded guilty to conspiring to provide material support to terrorists and was sentenced to eight and a half years in prison.

---

[25] al-Marri v. Pucciarelli, 534 F.3d 213, 221 (2008) (Traxler, J., concurring).

Kiyemba v. Obama, 555 F.3d 1022, vacated, 130 S. Ct. 1235 (2010)

In October 2008, a federal district court ordered the release into the United States of several Guantanamo detainees who were no longer considered enemy combatants but who could not be returned to their home country (China) because of the likelihood they would be subjected to torture there, finding that the political branches' plenary authority in the immigration context did not contravene the petitioners' entitlement to an effective remedy to their unauthorized detention.26 However, the D.C. Circuit panel stayed the district court's order pending appellate review,27 and subsequently reversed the district court's decision in the case of Kiyemba v. Obama, decided in February 2009. The majority held that although the constitutional writ of habeas enables Guantanamo detainees to challenge the legality of their detention, habeas courts lack authority (absent the enactment of an authorizing statute) to compel the transfer of a non-citizen detainee into the United States, even if that detainee is found to be unlawfully held and the government has been unable to effectuate his release to a foreign county. The Kiyemba panel's decision was primarily based on long-standing jurisprudence in the immigration context which recognizes that the political branches have plenary authority over whether arriving aliens may enter the United States. The majority of the panel also found that Guantanamo detainees were not protected by the Due Process Clause of the Constitution, as they are non-citizens held outside the U.S. and lack significant ties to the country. As discussed *supra*, the Supreme Court granted certiorari to review the *Kiyemba* ruling, but thereafter vacated the appellate court's opinion and remanded the case in light of the fact that several countries have agreed to resettle the petitioners. The D.C. Circuit must now review the ramifications of these new circumstances.

Kiyemba v. Obama, 561 F.3d 509 (D.C. Cir.) ("Kiyemba II"), cert. denied, 2010 WL 1005960, 78 USLW 3302 (U.S. Mar. 22, 2010)

In a second case entitled *Kiyemba v. Obama*, decided in April 2009, a D.C. Circuit panel considered *habeas* petitions by detainees who were no longer considered enemy combatants, and who sought to prevent their transfer to any country where they would likely face further detention or torture. The *Kiyemba II*

[26] In re Guantanamo Bay Detainee Litigation, 581 F. Supp. 2d 33 (D.D.C. 2008).

[27] Kiyemba v. Bush, No. 08-5424, 2008 WL 4898963, Order (D.C. Cir., October 20, 2008) (*per curiam*).

panel rejected the government's argument that the MCA stripped the court of jurisdiction to hear claims related to the petitioners' proposed transfer. The panel interpreted *Boumediene* as invalidating the MCA's court-stripping provisions with respect "to all *habeas* claims brought by Guantanamo detainees, not simply with respect to so-called 'core' *habeas* claims" relating to the legality of the petitioners' detention. However, the panel held that an executive branch determination that a detainee will not be tortured if transferred to a particular country is binding on the court, and a *habeas* court may not second-guess this assessment. The circuit panel also reversed a district court ruling that required the government to provide 30 days' notice to detainees' counsel before any proposed transfer. As a result of this ruling, the detainees' ability to challenge their proposed transfer from Guantanamo may be quite limited. On March 22, 2010, the Supreme Court denied a petition for writ of certiorari to review the appellate court's ruling.

Bismullah v. Gates, 551 F.3d 1068 (D.C. Cir. 2009)[28]

This case concerned the continuing availability of DTA review procedures in light of the Supreme Court's ruling in *Boumediene v. Bush* that the constitutional privilege of *habeas corpus* extends to non-citizen detainees held at Guantanamo. As discussed *supra*, following the Supreme Court's ruling in *Gates v. Bismullah*, the D.C. Circuit reinstated two earlier rulings concerning the scope of judicial review of CSRT determinations available under the DTA. The government subsequently petitioned for a rehearing of the case, arguing that the Supreme Court's ruling in *Boumediene* effectively nullified the review system established by the DTA, as Congress had not intended for detainees to have two judicial forums in which to challenge their detention. The D.C. Circuit granted the government's motion for rehearing, and in *Bismullah v. Gates*, a three-judge panel held that, in light of the Supreme Court's ruling in *Boumediene* restoring detainees' ability to seek *habeas* review of the legality of their detention, the appellate court no longer had jurisdiction over petitions for review filed pursuant to the DTA.

[28] A more detailed discussion of the *Bismullah* case is found in CRS Report RL33 180, *Enemy Combatant Detainees: Habeas Corpus Challenges in Federal Court*, by Jennifer K. Elsea and Michael John Garcia.

Al-Bihani v. Obama, 590 F.3d 866 (D.C. Cir. 2010)

In January 2010, a three-judge panel of the D.C. Circuit Court of Appeals considered the scope of the government's detention authority under the AUMF in the case of *Al-Bihani v. Obama*. In an opinion supported in full by two members of the panel,[29] the appellate court endorsed the definitional standard for the Executive's detention authority that had initially been asserted by the Bush Administration; namely, that the President may detain those persons who are "part of or supporting Taliban or al Qaeda forces, or associated forces that are engaged in hostilities against the United States or its coalition partners."[30] The petitioner claimed that he was merely a cook for a military unit associated with the Taliban during its conflict with the Northern Alliance in Afghanistan, and argued that his detention is inconsistent with the law of war and, by extension, the AUMF. While the panel concluded that either support for or membership in an AUMF targeted organization may be independently sufficient to justify detention, it declined "to explore the outer bounds of what constitutes sufficient support or indicia of membership to meet the detention standard." It did, however, note that this standard would permit the detention of a "civilian contractor" who "purposefully and materially supported" an AUMF-targeted organization through "traditional food operations essential to a fighting force and the carrying of arms." Notwithstanding the government's reliance on the law of war to interpret the scope of the AUMF and seemingly in conflict with Supreme Court discussion of the issue in *Hamdi*, the panel rejected the idea that the international law of war has any relevance to the courts' interpretation of the scope of the detention power conferred by the AUMF.

The panel also held that the procedural protections afforded in *habeas* cases involving wartime detainees do not need to mirror those provided to persons in the traditional criminal law context.

The government need only support its authority to detain using a "preponderance of evidence" standard. The panel also held that *habeas* courts assessing the validity of a petitioner's detention may properly consider hearsay evidence proffered by the government.

---

[29] A third member of the panel issued a separate opinion concurring with the majority's judgment. However, the opinion did not clearly endorse the majority's view as to scope of the Executive's detention authority. *See* Al-Bihani v. Obama, 590 F.3d 866, 883-885 (D.C. Cir. 2010) (Williams, J., concurring) (arguing that petitioner was detainable on account of being "part of" an AUMF-targeted organization, but not deciding whether a person could be detained on account of "support" for a targeted organization that he was not also a "part of").

[30] This standard had been slightly circumscribed by the Obama Administration, which had endorsed a standard that requires support to be "substantial."

Rasul v. Myers, 563 F.3d 527 (D.C. Cir. 2009) (per curiam), cert. denied, 130 S.Ct. 1013 (U.S. Dec. 14, 2009)

Four British nationals formerly detained at Guantanamo sued the Secretary of Defense and various military officers for damages, alleging that their treatment while in U.S. military custody violated their rights under the Fifth and Eighth Amendments to the Constitution, the Geneva Conventions, and other provisions of law. The district court dismissed the *Bivens*[31] claims on the basis of qualified immunity, holding that the officers could not reasonably be expected to have anticipated that the plaintiffs, as aliens held overseas, would be entitled to rights under the U.S. Constitution.[32] The D.C. Circuit twice affirmed,[33] interpreting *Boumediene* (on remand) as "disclaim[ing] any intention to disturb existing law governing the extraterritorial reach of any constitutional provisions, other than the Suspension Clause,"[34] which, in the circuit court's view, appears to mean that those detained at Guantanamo have no rights under the Constitution (other than the right to petition for *habeas corpus*). It rested its holding, however, on its analysis of qualified immunity under *Bivens*, agreeing with the lower court that even if the Constitution does provide some protections to the plaintiffs, the defendants were protected by qualified immunity. Even were this not so clear, the D.C. Circuit noted a "special factor" precludes extending a *Bivens* remedy to plaintiffs; namely, the "[t]he danger of obstructing U.S. national security policy."[35]

Having found that the claims for damages were barred by the Federal Tort Claims Act, the circuit court did not address whether *Boumediene*'s holding invalidating section 7 of the MCA encompassed only the portion of the provision that stripped courts of jurisdiction over *habeas* claims, or whether the language eliminating other causes of action against the government had also been

---

[31] Bivens v. Six Unknown Agents of Fed. Bureau of Narcotics, 403 U.S. 388 (1971) (providing for cause of action in tort for violation of certain constitutional rights).

[32] Rasul v. Rumsfeld, 414 F. Supp. 2d 26 (D.D.C. 2006).

[33] Rasul v. Myers, 512 F.3d 644 (D.C. Cir. 2008) ("Rasul I") was vacated by the Supreme court and remanded for reconsideration in light of *Boumediene*. 129 S.Ct. 763 (2008) Rasul v. Myers, 563 F.3d 527 (D.C. Cir. 2009) ("Rasul II") reinstated the earlier opinion but limited its scope to rest the holding on qualified immunity without adjudicating the constitutional questions. The appellate court reversed a holding by the district court that would have enabled plaintiffs to pursue claims based on the Religious Freedom Restoration Act (RFRA), 42 U.S.C. §§ 2000bb *et seq*.

[34] *Rasul II*, 563 F.3d at 529.

[35] *Id*. at 532 & n.5.

invalidated.[36] District court judges have uniformly held that the language eliminating causes of action other than *habeas corpus* survived Boumediene.[37]

District Court Opinions

The following section discusses significant rulings made by the federal district courts that are the subject of ongoing *habeas* litigation.

Recent District Court Rulings Concerning Scope of Executive Detention Authority

In the aftermath of the Supreme Court's decision in *Boumediene*, federal *habeas* courts reviewing claims raised by Guantanamo detainees have reached differing conclusions regarding the scope of the Executive's detention authority under the AUMF and the law of war. Judge Richard J. Leon, the first district court judge to rule on this issue post -*Boumediene*, applied the standard employed by the Department of Defense (DOD) in 2004 CSRT proceedings, which authorized the detention of those who were "part of or supporting Taliban or al Qaeda forces, or associated forces that are engaged in hostilities against the United States or its coalition partners ... [including] any person who has committed a belligerent act or has directly supported hostilities in aid of enemy armed force."[38] More recent rulings by district courts have taken a more limited view of the Executive's detention authority. A few district court judges have held that the Executive has authority to detain persons who were "part of" or "substantially supported" Al Qaeda, the Taliban, or associated forces, so long as those terms are understood to

[36] 28 U.S.C. § 2241(e)(2), provides that [n]o court ... shall have jurisdiction to hear or consider any other action against the United States or its agents relating to any aspect of the detention, transfer, treatment, trial, or conditions of confinement of an alien who is or was detained by the United States and has been determined by the United States to have been properly detained as an enemy combatant or is awaiting such determination.

[37] Al-Zahrani v. Rumsfeld, No. 09-0028, slip op. at 7 (D.D.C. 2010) (citing Al-Adahi v. Obama, 596 F. Supp. 2d 111, 119 (D.D.C. 2009); Khadr v. Bush, 587 F. Supp. 2d 225, 235-36 (D.D.C. 2009); *In re* Guantanamo Bay Detainee Litig., 577 F. Supp. 2d 312, 314 (D.D.C. 2008); *In re* Guantanamo Bay Detainee Litig., 570 F. Supp. 2d 13, 18 (D.D.C. 2008)). *See also* Kiyemba v. Obama, 561 F.3d 509, 512 n.1 (D.C. Cir. 2009) (in *habeas* case, noting that *Boumediene* "referred to § 7 without specifying a particular subsection of § 224 1(e) but its discussion of the Suspension Clause clearly indicates it was referring only to that part of § 7 codified at § 224 1(e)(1)")).

[38] Boumediene v. Bush, 583 F.Supp.2d 133 (D.D.C. 2008) (Leon, J.).

include only those persons who were members of the enemy organizations' *armed forces* at the time of capture.[39] Other judges have held that the Executive has authority under the AUMF and the law of war to detain persons who were "part of" the Taliban, Al Qaeda, or associated forces, but lacks authority to detain non-members who provide "support" to such organizations (though such support may be considered when determining whether a detainee was "part of" one of these groups).[40] As discussed *supra*, in *Al-Bihani v. Obama* a three-judge D.C. Circuit panel endorsed the definitional standard used by Judge Leon to assess the Executive's detention authority. It is possible that this issue will be the subject of further litigation, either before the circuit court sitting *en banc* or the Supreme Court.

Several (though not all) district court judges have concluded that an individual's continuing threat to U.S. security is not a relevant consideration in determining whether he may be lawfully detained under the AUMF.[41] At least one district court judge has expressly held that "the President is authorized to detain [a properly designated enemy belligerent] for the duration of the conflict in Afghanistan, even if [he] poses no threat of returning to the field of battle."[42] However, this conclusion has not been endorsed by every district court judge who has considered the issue.[43]

Al Maqaleh v. Gates, 604 F. Supp. 2d 205 (D.D.C. 2009)

In April 2009, District Court Judge John D. Bates found in the case of *Al Maqaleh v. Gates* that the constitutional writ of *habeas* may extend to non-Afghan

---

[39] Gherebi v. Obama, 609 F.Supp.2d 43 (D.D.C. 2009) (Walton, J.); Al-Adahi v. Obama, 2009 WL 2584685 (D.D.C. August 21, 2009) (Kessler, J.).

[40] Hamlily v. Obama, 616 F.Supp.2d 63 (D.D.C. 2009) (Bates, J.); Mattan v. Obama, 618 F.Supp.2d 24 (D.D.C. 2009) (Lamberth, C.J.). In assessing whether an individual was "part of" the Taliban, Al Qaeda, or associated forces, several *habeas* judges have considered whether "the individual functions or participates within or under the command structure of the organization—i.e. whether he receives and executes orders or directions." *Hamlily*, 616 F.Supp.2d at 75; Al Odah v. United States, 648 F.Supp.2d 1, 7 (D.D.C. 2009) (Kollar-Kotelly, J.) (citing *Hamlily*); Awad v. Obama, 646 F.Supp.2d 20, 23 (D.D.C. 2009) (Robertson, J.) (same).

[41] Al-Adahi v. Obama, No. 05-280, 2010 WL 811280, at *4 (Kessler, J.); *Awad*, 646 F.Supp.2d at 24; Anam v. Obama, No. 04-1194, 2010 WL 58965, at *14 (D.D.C. Jan. 6, 2010) (Hogan, J.) (upholding detention of petitioner, despite finding that he did not pose a continuing threat to the United States.)

[42] *Al-Adahi*, 2010 WL 811280, at *4.

[43] *See* Basardh v. Obama, 612 F.Supp.2d 30, 34 (D.D.C. 2009)(Huvelle, J.) ("the AUMF does not authorize the detention of individuals beyond that which is necessary to prevent those individuals from rejoining the battle").

detainees currently held by the United States at the Bagram Theater Internment Facility in Afghanistan, when those detainees had been captured outside of Afghanistan but were transferred to Bagram for long-term detention as enemy combatants. Judge Bates held that the circumstances surrounding the detention of the petitioners in *Al Maqaleh* were "virtually identical to the detainees in *Boumediene*—they are [non-U.S.] citizens who were ... apprehended in foreign lands far from the United States and brought to yet another country for detention."[44] Applying the factors discussed in *Boumediene* as being relevant to a determination of the extraterritorial scope of the writ of *habeas corpus*, Judge Bates concluded that the writ extended to three of the four petitioners at issue in *Al Maqaleh*, who were not Afghan citizens. The constitutional writ was not found to extend to a fourth petitioner who was an Afghan citizen, however, because review of his *habeas* petition could potentially cause friction with the Afghan government.[45] This ruling has been appealed. Presuming that the ruling is upheld, it could have significant ramifications for U.S. detention policy, as at least some foreign detainees held outside the United States or Guantanamo could seek review of their detention by a U.S. court.

On September 14, 2009, the DOD announced modifications to the administrative process used to review the status of aliens held at Bagram, which would afford detainees greater procedural rights. The modified process does not contemplate judicial review of administrative determinations regarding the detention of persons at Bagram.[46]

CRIMINAL CASES

Although numerous cases have been brought in federal civilian court involving persons who allegedly engaged in terrorist activity, relatively few involve persons who were captured abroad by U.S. forces during operations

---

[44] *Al Maqaleh*, 604 F. Supp. 2d at 209 (D.D.C. 2009).

[45] *Id.* at 229-230.

[46] Under this new system, detainees would undergo a case review within 60 days of incarceration, with periodic review occurring roughly every six months thereafter. Further, U.S. military members shall act as personal representatives to assist detainees during the review process. Letter from Phillip Carter, Dep. Asst. Sec. Defense for Detainee Policy, to Sen. Carl Levin, Chairman of Sen. Armed Serv. Comm., July 14, 2009, available at http://www.scotusblog.com/wp/ wp-content/uploads/2009/09/US-Bagram-brief-9-14-09.pdf; Gerry J. Gilmore, "Bagram Detention Facility to Implement Case Review Panels," *American Forces Press Service*, September 14, 2009, http://www.defenselink.mil/news/newsarticle.aspx?id=55831.

against either Al Qaeda or the Taliban, and only one case has been tried in civilian court involving a person involved in the September 11, 2001, terrorist attacks.

This section discusses notable rulings made in criminal cases involving Zacharias Moussaoui, who was tried and convicted for his role in the September 11, 2001, terrorist attacks, but was never officially designated as an "enemy combatant"; John Walker Lindh, thus far the only person captured abroad and tried and convicted in federal civilian court for belligerent activities occurring on the Afghan battlefield; and Ahmed Khalfan Ghailani, a suspect in the 1998 African Embassy bombings who was incarcerated at Guantanamo and charged at a military commission, but was later transferred to the Southern District of New York for trial on terrorism charges. Ghailani is the only Guantanamo prisoner to have been transferred for civilian trial in the United States.

Moussaoui Litigation

Zacharias Moussaoui, a French citizen, was arrested by immigration authorities for overstaying his visa after he raised suspicions at a Minnesota flight school where he was enrolled. Less than a month after he was taken into custody, a group of Al Qaeda terrorists carried out the September 11, 2001, attacks, and Moussaoui was charged in connection with the conspiracy to commit those attacks. On January 7, 2002, after Moussaoui's arraignment, the Department of Justice (DOJ) imposed Special Administrative Measures (SAMs) to prevent his communication with other terrorists. Moussaoui was permitted unmonitored attorney/client and consular communications and mail, and monitored communications with others. The court also issued a protective order under the Classified Information Procedures Act (CIPA; 18 U.S.C. app. 3, § 3), which permitted defense counsel to access classified information, but did not permit Moussaoui to receive such information unless the government consented or the judge determined that it was necessary to protect his right to prepare a defense.

After a competency hearing in which the judge explained that the lack of personal access to classified information could impede Moussaoui's ability to defend himself without counsel appropriately cleared for access to such information, the judge permitted the defendant to proceed *pro se*, and appointed the public defenders who had been assigned to the case to act as standby counsel. After Moussaoui refused to cooperate with his appointed lawyers, the judge replaced some of them, but ultimately concluded that Moussaoui was unlikely to approve any court- appointed attorneys, and also held that he was not entitled to unmonitored access to "advisory counsel" of his choice. Despite Moussaoui's rejection of virtually all efforts by standby counsel to assist him, the lawyers continued to file motions on his behalf, including motions seeking relief from the SAMs or to revoke his *pro se* status on the grounds that he was not in a position to take advantage of exculpatory information in the government's possession. Moussaoui attempted to plead guilty in July, 2002, but was unwilling to admit to the facts necessary to support the plea and withdrew it.

Moussaoui then sought access to several persons held overseas by the government as enemy combatants who might provide information that would be useful to his defense by testifying that Moussaoui was not involved in the September 11 attacks. (The government had advanced theories that Moussaoui was the intended "20th hijacker" or pilot of a fifth plane intended to target the White House, whose participation in the actual attack was thwarted due to his incarceration, and that Moussaoui's refusal to provide agents information about the plot that might have prevented the attacks from taking place contributed to the deaths of the several thousand victims, a factor relevant to death penalty eligibility. Moussaoui claimed to be part of a plan for subsequent terrorist operations and to have had no knowledge regarding the September 11 plot.) The government offered to provide redacted summaries of reports presumably based on intelligence interrogations of the enemy combatant witnesses,[47] but the judge rejected the proffered substitutions as possibly unreliable and inadequate to protect Moussaoui's Sixth Amendment right to compulsory process.

The government appealed the district court's order requiring the government to make three of the requested enemy combatant witnesses available for deposition to be conducted by remote video. The United States Court of Appeals for the Fourth Circuit affirmed the district court's holding that that the enemy combatants in question could be reached through judicial process (directed at their custodians) for the purpose of providing testimony and that their testimony would be relevant to the case, but reversed the order for depositions and the sanctions the court had imposed for the government's refusal to comply.[48] The appellate court

---

[47] The exact nature of the information and its acquisition by the government is obscured by the many redactions in the reported opinions.

[48] United States v. Moussaoui, 382 F.3d 453, 456-57 (4th Cir. 2004) ("*Moussaoui II*"). In "*Moussaoui I*," 333 F.3d 509, 517 (4th Cir. 2003), the circuit court dismissed the appeal of the discovery order as unripe and remanded for the government to propose substitutions for the witness testimony similar to those available under CIPA. (CIPA applies to the production of documents during discovery but does not address witnesses). The district court imposed sanctions on remand after the government refused to make the enemy combatant witnesses available for deposition. The judge rejected the parties' proposal for an order of dismissal, the ordinary sanction under CIPA in cases in which the government declines to provide classified information the court has determined is necessary for the defense. Instead, she dismissed the death notice on the grounds that the witnesses could provide testimony that might preclude a

held that substitutions for depositions could be prepared that would provide substantially the same ability to prepare a defense, although it agreed with some of the objections the district court had articulated regarding the government's proposed substitutions. The majority viewed the intelligence reports as possessing adequate indicia of reliability because they were produced through methods designed to produce accurate analyses of foreign intelligence.[49] Consequently, the court remanded the case to the district court with instructions to prepare substitutions for the deposition testimony by a process involving collaboration with the parties,[50] noting that adequate jury instructions would be necessary in some cases to permit the jury to assess the reliability of the evidence.

In the meantime, the district court revoked Moussaoui's *pro se* privilege for his continued submission of improper filings, some of which contained veiled or overt threats, political statements with no relevance to the case, attempts at communicating to persons overseas, and insulting language, despite repeated warnings that such conduct would result in sanctions. After the Supreme Court denied certiorari with respect to the appellate court's ruling on his right to depose enemy combatant witnesses in the custody of the United States, Moussaoui again decided, over his counsel's objections, to plead guilty as an apparent tactic to avoid the death penalty. After a hearing in which Moussaoui demonstrated to the court's satisfaction that he understood a guilty plea would result in forfeiting his right to appeal based on any violation of his constitutional rights that might have occurred prior to the plea, the court accepted his plea. Moussaoui admitted to the government's allegations, including some he had previously denied, and signed the statement of facts supporting the guilty plea, adding the designation of "20th Hijacker" below his signature. During the sentencing phase, Moussaoui claimed that his mission on September 11 was to have been piloting a commercial airliner

---

jury from finding Moussaoui eligible for the death penalty. Because the testimony could exonerate Moussaoui of involvement in the September 11 attacks, the district court prohibited the government "from making any argument, or offering any evidence, suggesting that the defendant had any involvement in, or knowledge of, the September 11 attacks." United States v. Moussaoui, 282 F. Supp. 2d 480, 327 (E.D. Va. 2003). Evidence that would have been excluded under the order included cockpit voice recordings, video footage showing the collapse of the World Trade Center Towers, and photographs of victims.

[49] 382 F.3d at 487 n. 31. Judge Gregory noted in dissent that such information may be reliable for intelligence purposes and yet omit relevant information that might be helpful to the defense because such information was not deemed to have any actionable foreign intelligence value. *Id.* at 488, n. 6.

[50] As noted by a dissenting judge of the appellate panel, the procedures crafted by the majority deviate from CIPA procedures by having the district judge, rather than the government, prepare the substitutions for the potential testimony, arguably making the district court judge an advocate in the proceedings. 382 F.3d. at 484-85 (Gregory, J., concurring in part and dissenting in part).

into the White House, although statements by enemy combatant witnesses introduced by the government contradicted that claim, along with some other allegations Moussaoui had admitted as true. In the bifurcated sentencing proceeding, the jury found Moussaoui to be eligible to receive the death penalty but declined to impose it, sentencing him instead to life in prison.

Just days after receiving his sentence, Moussaoui filed a motion to withdraw his guilty plea, claiming that his understanding of the American legal system had been "completely flawed" and asking for a new trial "[b]ecause I now see that it is possible that I can receive a fair trial ... even with Americans as jurors and that I can have the opportunity to prove that I did not have any knowledge of and was not a member of the plot to hijack planes and crash them into buildings on September 11, 2001."[51] He then appealed the court's denial of his motion for a new trial, arguing among other things that his plea was not voluntary as a matter of law because of district court rulings that violated his constitutional rights, and that it was not knowing because he did not have access to classified information in the government's possession that contradicted the government's theory of the case. Finding that his guilty plea was entered with full knowledge and understanding of its ramifications and that his objections to constitutional claims were waived, the circuit court affirmed. The circuit court reviewed the procedural history regarding Moussaoui's access to classified information because these claims were relevant to the adequacy of the plea and were therefore not waived for purposes of appeal, but reiterated its earlier view that adequate substitutions under CIPA would have protected Moussaoui's rights had the CIPA process not been cut short by the guilty plea. Moreover, it noted that CIPA information had been made available during the sentencing phase for establishing death-eligibility factors, and that not only did Moussaoui make no effort to withdraw his plea upon receiving the information, but he contradicted the supposedly exculpatory statements at trial. Finally, the circuit court rejected Moussaoui's contention that plain error had resulted in the jury's false belief that the only sentencing options available to them were the death penalty or life imprisonment without possibility of parole, in violation of his right to have his sentence decided by the jury, on the basis that Moussaoui had requested the jury be instructed that the sentencing options were limited as part of an apparently successful strategy to avoid the death penalty.

[51] Moussaoui v. Obama, 591 F.3d 263, 278 (4th Cir. 2010).

United States v. Lindh, 227 F. Supp. 2d 565 (E.D. Va. 2004)

John Walker Lindh, a U.S. citizen, was captured in Afghanistan and charged with ten counts of supplying services to the Taliban under various statutes. He moved to have the charges dismissed, arguing, *inter alia* that he was entitled to combatant immunity as part of the Taliban. While the judge refused to accept the government's argument that the President's designation of Lindh as an "unlawful combatant" was not subject to second-guessing by the court, he nevertheless concluded that the Taliban is not entitled to combatant immunity under international law and rejected the defense.[52]

Lindh was also unsuccessful in his bid to avoid the government's request for a protective order covering unclassified but sensitive information as well as classified information that the government had concluded was subject to discovery by the defendant.[53] At issue was whether the defendant could adequately prepare a defense given the government's proposal to restrict certain information from the government's redacted reports of relevant interviews with detainees held at Guantanamo. Rule 16(d) of the Federal Rules for Criminal Procedure permits the court to restrict discovery with respect to any information for good cause, including cases where the government claims the protection of such information is vital to the national security. The court found good cause to issue a protective order to prohibit the public dissemination of the detainee interview reports, which would serve to prevent Al Qaeda members from learning "the status of, the methods used in, and the information obtained from the ongoing investigation of the detainees."[54] Lindh objected to the order on the basis that it would burden his ability to prepare for trial by requiring the pre-screening of investigators and expert witnesses before he would be permitted to disclose unclassified information to them, which he argued could reveal his defense strategy to the prosecution. The judge found the needs of both parties could be accommodated by amending the proposed order to require investigators or expert witnesses for the defense to sign a memorandum of understanding, under oath, promising not to disclose information provided under the order, rather than requiring pre-screening. Lindh also objected to the proposed protective order because he believed it would impair his ability to use the media to influence

[52] United States v. Lindh, 212 F. Supp. 2d 541, 557-58 (E.D. Va. 2002). The judge also rejected Lindh's contention that media publicity had rendered a fair trial for him impossible, at least in that particular court, and that the International Economic Emergency Powers Act ("IEEPA") (50 U.S.C. § 1701 et seq.) regulations he was charged with violating were not valid.

[53] United States v. Lindh, 198 F. Supp. 2d 739 (E.D. Va. 2002).

[54] *Id.* at 742.

public opinion, as he contended the government had done. Noting that the "[d]efendant has no constitutional right to use the media to influence public opinion concerning his case so as to gain an advantage at trial" under either the Sixth Amendment right to a public trial or the public's First Amendment right to a free press,[55] the judge rejected the argument, but cautioned that information that turned out to be relevant and material to the trial as the case progressed might eventually require unsealing to further those rights.[56]

Prior to the beginning of the merits phase of the trial, Lindh struck a plea deal with prosecutors, admitting to one count of carrying an explosive during the commission of a felony, and was sentenced to 20 years' imprisonment.

United States v. Ghailani, No. S10 98 Crim. 1023 (S.D.N.Y.)

Alleged Al Qaeda member Ahmed Khalfan Ghailani was indicted in 1998 and charged with conspiracy to kill Americans abroad in connection with the bombing the United States Embassies in Nairobi, Kenya, and Dar es Salaam, Tanzania. He was arrested in Pakistan in 2004 and turned over to U.S. custody to be held and interrogated at an undisclosed site abroad by Central Intelligence Agency (CIA) officials. In 2006, he was transferred to DOD custody and held as an enemy combatant at Guantanamo. He was charged before a military commission for his role in one of the embassy bombings, but the charges were later withdrawn so that he could be transferred to the Southern District of New York to be tried on the earlier indictment. The transfer occurred in May 2009.

Ghailani moved for an injunction or other relief against the Secretary of Defense to prevent the reassignment of the military defense attorneys who had been detailed to serve as his defense counsel before the military commission. Ghailani urged the court to order the government to permit the two officers to act as his appointed counsel in federal court, arguing that depriving him of the assistance of the counsel he had grown to trust amounted to a violation of his Sixth Amendment right to the effective assistance of counsel.

The government urged the court to decline to adjudicate the motion or grant relief based on the political question doctrine, arguing that the assignment of military officers to particular duties is the prerogative of the executive branch alone. The judge did not think the political question doctrine prevented his consideration of the matter, since he was not considering the propriety of the

[55] *Id.* at 743.
[56] *Id.* at 744.

reassignment as much as he was assessing the impact of the decision on the defendant's rights, but ultimately denied the motion, holding that an indigent defendant's right to appointed representation does not mean the right to continuous representation by counsel of his choice.[57]

Ghailani has also filed a motion for dismissal of his indictment based on his claim that the government violated his Sixth Amendment right to a speedy trial. In connection with this motion, Ghailani sought discovery of documents in the government's possession that demonstrate the government delayed his prosecution from 2004 until his transfer to New York for reasons other than national security. Rule 16 of the Federal Rules for Criminal Procedure permits discovery of items "within the government's custody, possession, or control" that are material to the case, excluding documents that were prepared by government attorneys or agents that constitute work product connected to the prosecution. The judge excluded one document specifically requested by the defendant as attorney work product, but approved a more general request for information relating to the reasons behind the timing of Ghailani's transfer for trial based on a Supreme Court ruling that makes the "reason for delay" one part of the test for determining whether charges must be dismissed for failure to provide a speedy trial.[58] The judge defined the scope of "in the government's possession, custody, or control" as reaching beyond the officials of the U.S. Attorney's Office who had worked on the case to include higher-level DOJ officials who were not intimately involved in the case but were involved in the decision about where to prosecute Ghailani.

This requirement will not unduly burden the prosecution with unreasonable discovery requirements, according to the court, because the embassy bombing crime had "commanded the attention of the highest levels" of the government long before Ghailani was in American custody. Under these circumstances, high-level officials involved in the important decisions involving Ghailani's treatment can be included within the meaning of "government" in Rule 16.[59] Accordingly, the judge issued an order requiring production of documents held by the DOJ that are material to the case and not otherwise privileged under the rule.

---

[57] United States v. Ghailani, No. S10 98 Crim. 1023, slip op. at 30, 2009 WL 3853799, at *11-12 (S.D.N.Y. Nov. 18, 2009) (citing Morris v. Slappy, 461 U.S. 1, 14 (1983); Wheat v. United States, 486 U.S. 153, 159 (1988)).

[58] United States v. Ghailani, No. S10 98 Crim. 1023, slip op. at 7-8, 2010 WL 653269, at *2-3 (S.D.N.Y. Jan. 21, 2010) (citing Barker v. Wingo, 407 U.S. 514 (1972)).

[59] *Id.*, slip op. at 12, 2010 WL 653269, at *4.

In: New Developments in Human Rights
Editors: J. M. Bauer and C. P. Davies
ISBN 978-1-61324-316-9

Chapter 4

"DON'T ASK, DON'T TELL:" THE LAW AND MILITARY POLICY ON SAME-SEX BEHAVIOR

David F. Burrelli*
Military Manpower Policy

SUMMARY

In 1993, new laws and regulations pertaining to homosexuality and U.S. military service came into effect reflecting a compromise in policy. This compromise, colloquially referred to as "don't ask, don't tell," holds that the presence in the armed forces of persons who demonstrate a propensity or intent to engage in same-sex acts would create an unacceptable risk to the high standards of morale, good order and discipline, and unit cohesion which are the essence of military capability. Under this policy, but not the law, service members are not to be asked about nor allowed to discuss their "same-sex orientation." The law itself does not prevent service members from being asked about their sexuality. This compromise notwithstanding, the issue has remained politically contentious.

Prior to the 1993 compromise, the number of individuals discharged for homosexuality was generally declining. Since that time, the number of discharges for same-sex conduct has generally increased until 2001. However, analysis of

* Email: dburrelli@crs.loc.gov

these data shows no statistically significant difference in discharge rates for these two periods.

In recent years, several Members of Congress have expressed interest in amending "don't ask, don't tell." At least two bills would repeal the law and replace it with a policy of nondiscrimination on the basis of sexual orientation—H.R. 1283 and S. 3065—have been introduced in the 111th Congress.

On March 25, 2010, Secretary of Defense Robert M. Gates announced changes in the department's enforcement of the 1993 law. Under these changes, Secretary Gates said only a general or flag officer would have the authority to separate someone who had engaged in homosexual conduct, that information provided by a third party must be given under oath, and that the information given to certain individuals—lawyers, pyschotherapist, clergy, and domestic abuse counselors, for example—cannot be used in support of discharge proceedings.

RECENT DEVELOPMENTS

Two bills—H.R. 1283 and S. 3065[1]—have been introduced in the 111th Congress calling for the repeal of Section 654, title 10 United States Code (see the Appendix), which bars homosexual behavior and thereby prohibits gays, lesbians, and bisexuals from serving openly in the military. These bills would replace Section 654 with a nondiscriminatory policy based on "sexual orientation," which is defined differently in each bill, and differently from the existing definition in policy. On January 27, 2010, President Barack Obama stated his desire to work with Congress "to finally repeal the law that denies gay Americans the right to serve the country they love because of who they are."[2] The House Military Personnel Subcommittee, on March 3, 2010, and the Senate Armed Services Committee (SASC), on February 2 and March 18, 2010, have held hearings on the issue. During the February SASC hearing, Secretary of Defense Robert Gates and the Chairman of the Joint Chiefs of Staff, Admiral Michael Mullen, called for allowing homosexuals to serve openly and have ordered a review by the Department of Defense (DOD), that is expected to continue through the year.[3] On

---

[1] H.R. 1283, Rep. Ellen O. Tauscher (Rep. Patrick J. Murphy), March 3, 2009 and S. 3065, Sen. Joseph I. Lierberman, March 3, 2010.

[2] President Barack Obama, White House Office of the Press Secretary, Remarks of the President in the State of the Union Address, January 27, 2010.

[3] McMichael, William H., Mullen: Dropping 'don't ask' is 'the right thing to do,' *Navy Time*, February 15, 2010: 11, 14.

March 25, 2010, Secretary of Defense Robert M. Gates announced changes in the Department's enforcement of the 1993 law. Under these changes, Secretary Gates said only a general or flag officer would have the authority to separate someone who had engaged in homosexual conduct, that information provided by a third party must be given under oath, and that the information given to certain individuals—lawyers, pyschotherapist, clergy, and domestic abuse counselors, for example—can not be used in support of discharge proceedings.

BACKGROUND AND ANALYSIS

Early in the 1992 presidential campaign, then-candidate Bill Clinton commented that, if elected, he would "lift the ban" on homosexuals[4] serving in the military.[5] Existing policies had been in place since the Carter Administration and, historically speaking, gay, lesbian, and bisexual (same sex) behavior had not been tolerated in the military services. The issue drew heated debate among policymakers and the public at large. In response to congressional concerns, President Clinton put into place in early 1993, an interim compromise that allowed the Department of Defense an opportunity to study the issue and develop a "draft executive order" that would end discrimination on the basis of "sexual orientation." This interim compromise (announced on January 29, 1993) also provided Congress additional time to more fully exercise its constitutional authority under Article I, Section 8, clause 14, "To make rules for the Government and Regulation of the land and naval Forces," including the consideration of legislation and the holding of hearings on the issue. In announcing the interim agreement, the President noted that the Joint Chiefs of Staff agreed to remove questions regarding sexual orientation from the enlistment application.[6] One of the elements of the compromise was an agreement within the Congress not to immediately enact legislation that would have maintained the prior policy (of barring such individuals from service and continuing to ask recruits questions concerning their sexuality) until after the completion of a congressional review.[7]

---

[4] Usage of terms: Although the law and policy refer to 'homosexuality' and 'bisexuality' this report also refers, interchangeably, to "gays," "lesbians," and bisexuals.

[5] "[H]e elicited approving whoops when he said he would sign an executive order to eliminate discrimination based on sexual orientation in the US military." Wilkie, Curtis, Harvard tosses warmup queries to Clinton on eve of N.H. debate, *Boston Globe*, October 31, 1991: 22.

[6] President's News Conference, in *Public Papers of the Presidents of the United States, William J. Clinton, 1993, Book 1*, January 29, 1993: published 1994: 20.

[7] See *Congressional Record*, February 4, 1993, S2163-S2245.

The Senate and House Armed Services Committees (SASC and HASC) held extensive hearings on the issue in 1993. By May 1993, a congressional consensus appeared to emerge over what then-SASC chairman Sam Nunn described as a "don't ask, don't tell" approach. Under this approach, DOD would not ask questions concerning the sexual orientation of prospective members of the military, and individuals would be required to either keep a same-sex orientation to themselves, or, if they did not, they would be discharged if already in the service or denied enlistment/appointment if seeking to join the service.

On July 19, 1993, President Clinton announced his new policy. According to the President, the policy was to be made up of these essential elements:

> One, service men and women will be judged based on their conduct, not their sexual orientation. Two, therefore the practice ... of not asking about sexual orientation in the enlistment procedure will continue. Three, an open statement by a service member that he or she is a homosexual will create a rebuttable presumption that he or she intends to engage in prohibited conduct, but the service member will be given an opportunity to refute that presumption.... And four, all provisions of the Uniform Code of Military Justice will be enforced in an even-handed manner as regards both heterosexuals and homosexuals. And thanks to the policy provisions agreed to by the Joint Chiefs, there will be a decent regard to the legitimate privacy and associational rights of all service members.[8]

The Administration dubbed this policy, "don't ask, don't tell, don't pursue." It is noteworthy that the President did not mention "don't pursue" in the announcement of the policy on July 19, 1993. The inclusion of "don't pursue" (akin to a "don't investigate" stance advocated by gay rights groups) seemingly created a contradiction in the President's policy.[9] On the one hand, it maintained the notion of military necessity and privacy as found in the congressional compromise of "don't ask, don't tell," and then appeared to prevent efforts to enforce the regulations and laws which implement the broad policy by limiting the military's role via "don't pursue." This problem was discussed at hearings with then-Secretary of Defense Les Aspin. Secretary Aspin indicated that individuals could acknowledge their homosexuality without risking an investigation or

---

[8] President's News Conference, in *Public Papers of the Presidents of the United States, William J. Clinton, 1993, Book 1*, July 19, 1993: published 1994: 1111.

[9] According to a Senior Administration official " ... [W]e think that probably the most significant advance is heightened—no witch hunts, no pursuit policy. So I think it's fair to call this policy 'don't ask, don't tell, don't pursue.'" White House Briefing, Federal News Service, July 16, 1993.

discharge;[10] later he said that individual statements might not be credible grounds for investigating if the commander so decided, but, if investigated, such statements could be credible grounds for a discharge proceeding. Ultimately, the Secretary agreed that statements are grounds for investigations and possible discharge.

In these same hearings, held from March 29, 1993 through July 22, 1993, Senators raised numerous questions as to what behavior, if any, would justify the commencement of an investigation, and what grounds would justify an administrative discharge.[11] Since commanders and noncommissioned officers are not usually lawyers, many critics argued that such rules created legal technicalities that would prove dysfunctional in a military setting, and/or lead to an expansion of unpredictable court remedies.[12] At the same time, some argued that this outcome would not have displeased the Clinton Administration, even if it was not the original intent. This thesis held that implementation of the compromise policy

---

[10] "The previous policy was, ask, do not tell, investigate. The [proposed] policy is, do not ask, do not tell, do not investigate." Secretary of Defense, Les Aspin, U.S. Congress. Senate. Committee on Armed Services, Hearings, Policy Concerning Homosexuality in the Armed Forces, Senate Hearings 103-845, 103rd Cong., 2nd Sess., 1994: 746. "And even Secretary of Defense Les Aspin seemed a bit confused about the Clinton administration's new policy allowing homosexuals in the military, expressing doubt as to whether a single acknowledgment of homosexuality by a service member would constitute grounds for discharge... But grasping [the policy's] details could prove difficult, as Aspin himself demonstrated yesterday in response to a question from Sen. Jeff Bingaman (D-N.M.). The senator asked Aspin what would happen in the case of a homosexual soldier who reveals his sexual orientation to another soldier, who then reports the conversation to a commander. At first, Aspin said flatly that such a disclosure would not be grounds for dismissal.... But that brought a puzzled response from [committee chairman, Sen.] Nunn, who quoted Aspin as saying in his opening remarks that homosexual 'statements' were a form of prohibited conduct.... At that point, Aspin seemed to shift position." Lancaster, John, "Senators Find Clinton Policy on Gays in the Military Confusing," *Washington Post*, July 21, 1993: A12.

[11] An administrative discharge is designated as 'Honorable,' 'General,' or 'Other than Honorable,' and is provided by an executive decision reflecting the nature of the service performed by the member. A 'Bad Conduct' or 'Dishonorable' discharge can only be awarded via a court-martial during sentencing. As discussed in the section entitled "Discharge Statistics," the vast majority of gays, lesbians and bisexuals who are discharged receive administrative discharges and most of those are designated 'Honorable.'
See the hearings with then-Secretary of Defense Aspin and others following release of the July 19, 1993 Memorandum, U.S. Congress. Senate. Committee on Armed Services, Hearings, Policy Concerning Homosexuality in the Armed Forces, Senate Hearings 103-845, 103rd Cong., 2nd Sess., 1994: 700 et seq.

[12] "... [T]he complex nature of the compromise was evident in the puzzlement of committee members who described [the policy] as confusing, contradictory and an invitation to endless litigation in the courts." Lancaster, July 21, 1993. "Clinton interpreted this language at a news conference yesterday to mean that gay service personnel do 'not necessarily' have to remain in the closet. The senior Pentagon official acknowledged, however, that homosexuals probably will not be able to disclose their sexual orientation." Lancaster, John, "Policy Tosses Issue to Courts, Ambiguity Seen Leading to Protracted Litigation," *Washington Post*, July 20, 1993: A1.

would have encouraged judicial intervention and, thereby, would have provided a means to seek a judicial resolution asserting that the compromise was unconstitutional. These critics hypothesized that the Clinton Administration may have been following a strategy of tacitly implementing a muddled regulation, awaiting a legal challenge, then poorly defending the policy—thereby encouraging judicial intervention in finding the policy unconstitutional.[13] Administration officials insisted that President Clinton was merely trying to pursue a compromise that would take into account the concerns of the Congress and the military, but would also minimize discrimination against gays, lesbians and bisexuals.[14]

The policy announced by the Clinton Administration was based in large part, on sexual "orientation."[15] This term has generated problems concerning its practical definition. Some view a sexual "orientation" as non-behavioral while others do not exclude behavioral manifestations when speaking of a sexual "orientation." As will be discussed below, the Clinton Administration's use of the term was subject to varying interpretations.

The ambiguities in the Clinton Administration's interpretation of the policy, as well as conflicting legal rulings at the time, seemingly encouraged Congress to act. On November 30, 1993, the FY1994 National Defense Authorization Act was signed into law by President Clinton (P.L. 103- 160). Section 571 of the law, codified at 10 United States Code 654, describes homosexuality in the ranks as an "unacceptable risk ... to morale, good order, and discipline." The law codified the grounds for discharge as follows: (1) the member has engaged in, attempted to engage in, or solicited another to engage in a homosexual act or acts; (2) the member states that he or she is a homosexual or bisexual; or (3) the member has married or attempted to marry someone of the same sex. The law also stated that DOD would brief new entrants (accessions) and members about the law and policy on a regular basis. Finally, legislative language instructed that asking

---

[13] "Clinton was also asked by a reporter whether he would direct his Justice Department, which had days before been in ... [court] arguing for the ban, not to appeal the anti-ban ruling, but he did not answer.... Today, the Clinton Department of Justice has not only appealed the anti-ban ruling but is arguing in court that the government can discriminate on the basis of sexual orientation." Burr, Chandler, reprinted from *California Lawyer Magazine*, June, 1994.

[14] Secretary of Defense, Les Aspin stated, "The Chiefs understood that the Commander-in-Chief wanted to change the existing policy to end discrimination based solely on status. The President understood that it was extremely important that any changes occur in a way that maintained the high level of morale and unit cohesion which is so important for military readiness and effectiveness." Secretary of Defense, Les Aspin, (with DOD General Counsel, Jamie Gorelick), News Conference, Reuter Transcript Report, December 23, 1993: 1.

[15] U.S. Department of Defense, Secretary of Defense, *Memorandum for the Secretaries of the Army, Navy, Air Force, and Chairman of the Joint Chiefs of Staff*, July 19, 1993.

questions of new recruits concerning sexuality could be resumed—having been halted in January, 1993—on a discretionary basis. As such, this law represented a discretionary "don't ask, definitely don't tell" policy. Notably, the law contains no mention of "orientation." In many ways, this law contained a reiteration of the basic thrust of the pre-1993 policy (although it does not mention any restrictions regarding 'asking' about a person's sexuality).

On December 22, 1993, Secretary of Defense Aspin released new DOD regulations to implement the statute enacted the preceding month. Language in these regulations indicated that the Secretary was trying to incorporate both the restrictions in the law, and the President's desire to open military service "to those who have a homosexual orientation." The policy stated:

> A Service member may also be separated if he or she states that he or she is a homosexual or bisexual, or words to that effect. Such a statement creates a rebuttable presumption that the member engages in homosexual acts or has a propensity or intent to do so. The Service member will have the opportunity to rebut that presumption, however, by demonstrating that he or she does not engage in homosexual acts and does not have a propensity or intent to do so.[16]

However, the policy—not the law it ostensibly implemented—stated that "sexual orientation is considered a personal and private matter, and homosexual orientation is not a bar to service entry or continued service unless manifested by homosexual conduct." According to this statement of DOD regulations, "sexual orientation" was defined as "A sexual attraction to individuals of a particular sex." Following Aspin's resignation and the confirmation of William Perry as the new Secretary of Defense in February 1994, DOD reportedly accepted the recommendation of certain Senators to delete from DOD regulations the phrase, "homosexual orientation ... is not a bar to military service."[17]

---

[16] Office of the Assistant Secretary of Defense, (Public Affairs), News Release, December 22, 1993.

[17] U.S. Department of Defense, Office of the Assistant Secretary of Defense (Public Affairs), News Release, No. 605-93, *Directives Implementing the New DOD Policy on Homosexual Conduct in the Armed Forces*, December 22, 1993.

In its place, DOD inserted the statement:

> A person's sexual orientation is considered a personal and private matter, and is not a bar to service or continued service unless manifested by homosexual conduct.[18]

In addition, the definition of "sexual orientation" was modified:

> An abstract sexual preference for persons of a particular sex, as distinct from a propensity or intent to engage in sexual acts.[19]

The elusiveness of the definition of "orientation" is apparent. Under the Clinton Administration's original definition, "orientation" is a sexual attraction. Under the revised definition, it is an abstract preference. Other sources define sexual "orientation" to include overt sexual behavior.[20]

Current regulations, therefore, are based on conduct, including verbal or written statements. Since sexual "orientation" is "personal and private," DOD is not to ask and personnel are not to tell. Should an individual choose to make his or her homosexual "orientation" public—i.e., no longer private and personal, nor abstract—an investigation and discharge may well occur.

The ambiguous nature of the term "orientation" and its usage has not been without problems. In 1994, a Navy tribunal decided not to discharge Lt. Maria Zoe Dunning after she had made the statement "I am a lesbian" at a January 1993 rally. Her attorneys argued that she was not broadcasting her intentions to practice homosexuality but merely acknowledging her "sexual orientation." In the view of the reviewing officers, she had successfully rebutted the presumption that she would commit homosexual acts. Such a finding, if not inconsistent with the law and regulations, created a legal avenue via which homosexuals could announce

---

[18] U.S. Department of Defense, Office of the Assistant Secretary of Defense (P&R), *Qualification Standards for Enlistment, Appointment and Induction*, Directive1304.26, December 21, 1993, incorporating change 1, March 4, 1994: 9.

[19] U.S. Department of Defense, Assistant Secretary of Defense (P&R), Directive, *Enlisted Administrative Separations*, No. 1332.14, December 21, 1993, Incorporation Change March 4, 1994: 9. See Scarborough, Rowen, "White House cuts Phrase restricting gay discharges," *Washington Times*, February 10, 1994: A1, and, "Defense Policy on Gays Takes Effect," *Washington Post*, March 2, 1994.

[20] "Today's preferred terms and the term 'sexual orientation' itself have a variety of definitions in the literature but these generally comprise one or both of two components: a 'psychological' component and a 'behavioral' component. Not all definitions include both components, ..., definitions that include both of these components use either the conjunction 'and' or 'or' to join them." Sell, Randall L., "Defining and Measuring Sexual Orientation: A Review," *Archives of Sexual Behavior*, Vol. 26, No. 6, 1997: 646.

their sexuality without being discharged. Shortly afterward, the Department of Defense Office of the General Counsel released a memo,[21] in August 1995, addressing this issue:

> A member may not avoid the burden of rebutting the presumption merely by asserting that his or her statement of homosexuality was intended to convey only a message about sexual orientation ... and not to convey any message about propensity or intent to engage in homosexual acts. To the contrary, by virtue of the statement, the member bears the burden of proof that he or she does not engage in, and does not attempt, have a propensity, [n]or intend to engage in homosexual acts. If the member in rebuttal offers evidence that he or she does not engage in homosexual acts or have a propensity or intent to do so, the offering of the evidence does not shift the burden of proof to the government. Rather, the burden of proof remains on the member throughout the proceeding.[22]

As written, the law makes no mention of sexual "orientation," and is structured entirely around the concept of sexual "conduct" including statements concerning an individual's sexuality. Therefore, attempts to implement the statute, or analyze and evaluate it, in terms of "sexual orientation," have resulted in confusion and ambiguity, and are likely to continue to do so.

In recent years, several Members of Congress have expressed interest in amending "don't ask, don't tell," the latest of which would repeal the law and replace it with a policy of nondiscrimination on the basis of "sexual orientation." These bills, H.R. 1283 and S. 3065, have been introduced in the 111th Congress. The two bills vary in their definition of "sexual orientation." In H.R. 1283, "the term 'sexual orientation' means heterosexuality, homosexuality, or bisexuality, whether the orientation is real or perceived, and includes statements and consensual sexual conduct manifesting heterosexuality, homosexuality, or bisexuality." In S. 3065, "the term 'sexual orientation' means heterosexuality, homosexuality, or bisexuality, whether the orientation is real or perceived, and includes statements and consensual conduct that is not otherwise illegal manifesting heterosexuality, homosexuality, or bisexuality." These definitions differ from the current definition of "sexual orientation" as applied in the current regulations (see the previous two pages).

---

[21] Scarborough, Rowen, "Pentagon memo removes winning defense for gays," *Washington Times*, December 29, 1995: A3.

[22] U.S. Department of Defense, General Counsel, Memorandum for the General Counsels of the Military Departments, Judge Advocate General of the Army, Navy, and Air Force, and the Staff Judge Advocate to the Commandant of the Marine Corps, *Policy on Homosexual Conduct in the Armed Forces*, August 18, 1995.

On January 27, 2010, President Barack Obama stated his desire to work with Congress "to finally repeal the law that denies gay Americans the right to serve the country they love because of who they are."[23] During the 111th Congress, the House Military Personnel Subcommittee, on March 3, 2010, and the Senate Armed Services Committee, on February 2 and March 18, 2010, held hearings on the issue. (Also, it should be noted that the House Military Personnel Subcommittee held a hearing on July 23, 2008.) During the February SASC hearing, the Secretary of Defense, Robert Gates, and the Chairman of the Joint Chiefs of Staff, Admiral Michael Mullen, called for allowing homosexuals to serve openly and ordered a review, expected to continue through the year.[24] On March 25, 2010, Secretary Gates announced changes in the enforcement of "Don't Ask, Don't Tell" policy. According to the Department of Defense:

> "Today, I have approved a series of changes to the implementation of the current statute," Gates told reporters at a Pentagon news conference. "They were developed with full participation of the department's senior civilian and military leadership, and the changes are unanimously supported by Chairman Mullen, Vice Chairman Cartwright and the entire Joint Chiefs of Staff."
>
> The changes include:
>
> —Only a general or flag officer may separate an enlisted member believed at the conclusion of an investigation to have engaged in homosexual conduct. Under previous policy, a colonel—or for a captain in the Navy and Coast Guard—could order separation.
>
> —A revision in what's needed to begin an inquiry or a separation proceeding. Information provided by a third party now must be given under oath, "discouraging the use of overheard statements and hearsay," Gates said.
>
> —Certain categories of confidential information—such as information provided to lawyers, clergy and psychotherapists—no longer will be used in support of discharges. Information provided to medical personnel in furtherance of treatment, or to a public-health official in the course of seeing professional assistance for domestic or physical abuse also is excluded, as well as information obtained in the process of security-clearance investigations, in accordance with existing Pentagon policies.
>
> "These changes reflect some of the insights we have gained over 17 years of implementing the current law, including the need for consistency, oversight and clear standards," the secretary said. "I believe these changes represent an important improvement in the way the current law is put into practice—above all,

[23] President Barack Obama, White House Office of the Press Secretary, Remarks of the President in the State of the Union Address, January 27, 2010.

[24] McMichael, William H., Mullen: Dropping 'don't ask' is 'the right thing to do,' *Navy Time*, February 15, 2010: 11, 14.

by providing a greater measure of common sense and common decency to a process for handling what are difficult and complex issues for all involved." The military services have 30 days to conform their regulations to the changes. The new policies, however, took effect immediately upon Gates' announcement, meaning that they apply to all open cases, he said."[25]

DISCHARGE STATISTICS

Early reports in the media stated that since the implementation of the "don't ask, don't tell" policy in 1993, the number of discharges for homosexuality had increased.[26] According to data provided by DOD and reproduced in Table 1 from the early 1980s until Fiscal Year (FY) 1994, the number of personnel discharged for homosexual conduct (including statements) decreased. From FY1995 to FY200 1, the numbers rebounded, only to begin leveling off and decreased thereafter.

In April 1998, the Department of Defense released a review of the implementation of the "Policy on Homosexual Conduct." This review was instituted after complaints were aired that the increasing rate of discharges was a sign of "witch hunts" or anti-gay harassment. In its review, DOD concluded that "for the most part, the policy has been properly applied and enforced." DOD also stated:

> First, we found that the large majority of the discharges for homosexual conduct are based on the statements of service members who identify themselves as homosexual, as opposed to cases involving homosexual acts. The services believe that most of these statements— although not all of them—involve service members who voluntarily elect to disclose their sexual orientation to their peers, supervisors or commanders. The increase in the number of discharges for homosexual conduct since 1994 is attributable to this increase in statement cases. Discharges for homosexual acts and marriages has declined by 20% over the past three years [1994-1997]. Second, most of those discharged under the policy are junior personnel with very little time in the military, and most of the increase in discharges for homosexual conduct has occurred in this sector. The number of cases involving career service members is relatively small. Third, the great majority of discharges for homosexual conduct are uncontested and are processed

[25] Carden, Michael J., Army Sgt. 1st Class, Department of Defense, *News, American Forces Press Service*, March 25, 2010.

[26] Marquis, Christopher, "Discharges of Gay Troops Rise, And So Do Bias Incidents," *New York Times*, March 14, 2002.

administratively. Finally, more than 98% of all members discharged in Fiscal Year 1997 under the policy received honorable discharges. (Separation of enlisted members in their first 180 days of military service are generally uncharacterized.) Discharges under other than honorable conditions or courts-martial for consensual homosexual conduct are infrequent and have invariably involved aggravating circumstances or additional charges.[27]

With over a decade (1993-2009) of experience under the most recent changes instituted during the Clinton Administration, other explanations as to why individuals may announce their homosexuality or bisexuality have come forward. Most notable is the observation that the vast majority of those discharged for homosexuality are discharged because they made voluntary statements identifying themselves as gay, lesbian, bisexual or having such an "orientation." Some have speculated that these statements were made by service members so as to enable them to terminate their military obligations before their term of service was completed regardless of their sexual "orientation."[28]

Advocacy groups have claimed that anti-gay, lesbian and/or bisexual harassment has increased since the 1998 review, and that those discharges were

---

[27] U.S. Department of Defense, Office of the Assistant Secretary of Defense (Personnel and Readiness), Report to the Secretary of Defense, Review of the Effectiveness of the Application and Enforcement of the Department's Policy on Homosexual Conduct in the Military, April 1998: 3. This report stated that investigations could only be initiated after commanders receive specific and credible information concerning homosexual conduct and that inappropriate investigations occurred only in isolated instances.

[28] For example, see Moskos, Charles, "The Law Works—And Here's Why," *Army Times*, October 27, 2003: 62. "Homosexual separations for whatever reason are one-tenth of 1% of military personnel. Of those discharges, more than 80% are the result of voluntary 'statements' by service members. The number of discharges for homosexual 'acts' has declined over the past decade. Gay-rights advocates argue that the growth in discharges for statements is due largely to commanders improperly seeking out gays. Undoubtedly, that happens sometimes. Yet commanders also report being worried they might be accused of conducting 'witch hunts,' so they tend to process out an alleged homosexual only when a case of 'telling' is dumped in their laps. Let me offer another possible explanation. Whether you're gay or not, saying you are is now the quickest way out of the military with an honorable discharge. And identifying oneself as gay carries less stigma in our society than it once did. Consider that whites are proportionately three times more likely than blacks to be discharged for homosexuality. Are commanders singling out whites and investigating their sexual orientation? Highly unlikely. The stigma against homosexuality is stronger among blacks than whites, and thus blacks are less willing to declare they are gay. Gay advocates are quick to draw an analogy between the exclusion of homosexuals and racial segregation in the military. Many black soldiers find that analogy offensive." See also: Christenson, Sig, "Recruits Deny Lackland Harassment," *San Antonio Express-News*, February 7, 1999. These and other articles assert that claims of homosexuality can serve as a means of terminating a military obligation. "Mario isn't in the Army now. In March he left Fort Bragg with an honorable discharge. Some may find Mario's willingness to use his homosexuality as a means of shirking his commitment objectionable." Lamme, Robert, "Dazed in the Military," *The Advocate*, No. 673, January 24, 1995: 46.

brought about by "witch hunts," or invasive and unwarranted searching and discharging of gays, lesbians and bisexuals in the ranks.[29]

Although cases of aggressive investigations have been reported, the data would not appear to support the general use of such tactics. Recently, as the number of discharges has decreased, activists claim the Bush Administration was retaining gays, lesbians and bisexuals because of the need for manpower as a result of Operations Enduring Freedom and Iraqi Freedom. At the same time, activists bemoan the discharge of "mission-critical" linguists who were found to be gay, lesbian, or bisexual.[30] In 2005, the then-Assistant Secretary of Defense (Personnel and Readiness), Dr. David Chu, addressed the loss of these individuals. "We looked at the linguist issue, sir. My recollection of the numbers is that the majority of those people did not actually complete training. So they were not really linguists; they were in training when they violated the norms that Congress has set forth in statute and which is our responsibility to uphold."[31]

Critics contend that the activists are trying to have it both ways when "analyzing" data. From the data, it can be seen that such individuals who are discharged represent an extremely small percentage of the force. For instance, if it is assumed that gays, lesbians and bisexuals make up only 1.6% of the total active force of approximately 1.4 million,[32] there would be an estimated 22,400 gays,

---

[29] For example, see Langeland, Terje, "Gay Discharges on the Rise," INews, online at http://www.csindy.com/csindy/ 2002-05-30/news.html, May 30-June 15, 2002. "[Servicemembers Legal Defense Network] executive director, C. Dixon Osborn, said the numbers show the 'Don't Ask, Don't Tell' policy has failed... According to Dixon, the policy is being widely disregarded. 'The idea of 'Don't Ask, Don't Tell is a myth,' Osborn said. 'The Pentagon continues to ask and pursue and harass every day, which means that any of the promises that were made have gone by the wayside.'" See also, Myers, Steven Lee, "Gay Group's Study Finds Military Harassment Rising," *New York Times*, March 15, 1999. In a recent article, Sharon Alexander, an attorney for SLDN network offered the following possible explanations for the decrease in homosexual discharges, "First, there is a growing acceptance of gays serving in the military, she said, and some commanders, especially younger ones are reluctant to enforce a law they believe to be unfair.... It could be the case, Alexander said, that with a war on, commanders in the field either don't want to lose able-bodied soldiers or they simply don't have time to worry about enforcing 'Don't Ask, Don't Tell.' ... [A Pentagon spokesman, Lt.Col. Joe] Richard dismissed those explanations as a 'fanciful analysis' by opponents of the law. There's never been a concerted effort to go on witch hunts to identify gay soldiers, he said. 'It is only when they declare themselves or openly practice their sexual preference that we have no alternative but to begin the investigative process and make a determination as to whether or not they themselves are homosexual.'" Reinert, Patty, "Is The Military Out of Step?", *Houston Chronicle*, February 6, 2005.

[30] Hull, Anne, "How 'Don't Tell' Translates," *The Washington Post*, June 18, 2004: A1.

[31] U.S. Congress, House, Committee on Armed Services, Military Personnel Subcommittee, The Current Status of Military Recruiting and Retention, Hearings, 109th Cong., 1st Sess., July 19, 2005: 31.

[32] Data concerning the prevalence of homosexuality in society varies, but is reported to be approximately 1.6%. Smith, Tom W., "Adult Sexual Behavior in 1989: Number of Partners,

lesbians and bisexuals in uniform. In 2003, 653 or 2.9% of the estimated gays, lesbians and bisexuals in uniform were discharged for homosexual conduct. By 2009, that number dropped to 428, or approximately 1.9%.

More recently, an estimate reported by a "gay rights policy center" (the Williams Institute at the UCLA School of Law) suggested that homosexuals and bisexuals constitute 66,000 people in uniform.[33] CRS is unaware of any refereed journal or independent research that has sought to replicate, evaluate, or verify this claim. However, even, if it is accepted at face value, it shows that the armed forces are discharging an even smaller percentage of homosexuals. In 2009, the 428 discharged would account for 0.6% of the "estimated" gays in uniform and only approximately 0.0 17% percent of all active and Reserve Component personnel. In a total force of approximately 2,500,000 active and Reserve Component personnel, the administrative separation of such a small number is practically insignificant. Although many blame the "Don't Ask, Don't Tell" policy for these discharges, supporters counter that it is the very individuals discharged who are responsible for violating the law that Congress enacted and the military is required to enforce. Despite the true estimate of homosexuals in the military, it appears that many gays, lesbians, and bisexuals, who serve in silence under the current policy, are not discharged for homosexual behavior. Likewise, although gay advocates are critical of gays having to serve in silence, supporters of the Don't Tell law point out that the armed forces is "all-volunteer" and there is no constitutional right to serve in the military. In other words, gays know the law and are free to serve under these rules or abstain from joining if they can not abide by the rules.

Some have claimed that discharges decline during time of war, suggesting that the military ignores same-sex conduct when soldiers are most needed, only to "kick them out" once the crisis has passed.[34] It is notable that during wartime, the military services can, and have, instituted actions "to suspend certain laws relating

---

Frequency of Intercourse and Risk of AIDS," *Family Planning Perspectives*, Vol. 23, No. 3, May/June 1991: 104. The percentage of homosexual individuals in society varies according to definitions used and sampling methods. For a broader discussion, see CRS Report 93-52, *Homosexuals and U.S. Military Personnel Policy*, by David F. Burrelli, January 14, 1993: 12 (archived report reprinted in U.S. Congress, Senate, Hearings, Policy Concerning Homosexuality in the Armed Forces, S. Hrg. 103-845, 103rd Cong., 2nd Sess., March 29, 1993: 20-94.) CRS is unaware of any reliable empirical research supporting the frequent assertion that homosexuals account for 10% of the population. See Muir, J. Gordon, "Homosexuals and the 10% Fallacy," *Wall Street Journal*, March 31, 1993.

[33] O'Keefe, Ed, Eye Opener: Estimate: 66,000 gays in the military, *The Washington Post*, January 27, 2010.

[34] Lambert, Wade, and Stephanie Simon, "U.S. Military Moves to Discharge Some Gay Veterans of Gulf War," *Wall Street Journal*, July 30, 1991: B6.

to ... separation" that can limit administrative discharges. These actions, known as "stop-loss,"[35] allow the services to minimize the disruptive effects of personnel turnover during a crisis. However, administrative discharges for same sex conduct normally are *not* affected by stop-loss. It can be speculated that a claim of homosexuality during a crisis may be viewed skeptically, but under the policy would require an investigation. Stop-loss, as implemented requires an investigation to determine if the claim is bona fide or being used for some other reason, such as avoiding deployment overseas and/or to a combat zone. If, following an investigation, such a claim was found to be in violation of the law on homosexual conduct, the services could not use "stop-loss" to delay an administrative discharge.[36]

In practice, it is quite possible for an individual, during a crisis, to claim to be gay, lesbian or bisexual and to be deployed while awaiting the results of an investigation. Likewise, a claim made during a non-crisis situation would more likely be dealt with in a routine manner, leading to a discharge. Gay rights groups assert that commanders tend to be more reluctant to discharge someone during a crisis situation. They contend that differing treatment of gays during crisis and non-crisis situation creates a double standard. Likewise, commanders and others are often more skeptical of such claims made during a crisis.

According to an Army Reserve Component Unit Commander's Handbook,[37] homosexual conduct is one of many criteria necessitating "personnel action during the mobilization process." According to this document, if a discharge for homosexuality "has been requested and approved prior to the unit's receipt of alert notification, the member will be discharged prior to the unit's effective date of [active duty]." Further, if "discharge is requested but not yet approved, delayed entry will be requested ... pending final determination." Finally, if "discharge is not requested prior to the unit's receipt of alert notification, discharge is not authorized."

Some gay rights activists claim that this is proof that the military retains known gays, lesbians and bisexuals during a time of crisis/mobilization. This

---

[35] 10 U.S.C. 12305, Authority of President to suspend certain laws relating to promotion, retirement, and separation.

[36] U.S. Department of the Army, Information Paper, *Army Stop Loss/Stop Movement Program*, March 11, 2004, "Soldiers normally not subject to the Army Stop Loss/Stop Movement Program[:] Those soldiers in violation of the Army's homosexual conduct policy." Tice, Jim, "Stop-Loss Extends to All on Active Duty," *Army Times*, February 25, 1991: 16. Those not covered by stop-loss include "soldiers eligible for disability retirement or separation, dependency, hardship, pregnancy, misconduct, punitive actions, unsatisfactory performance and homosexuality."

[37] U.S. Army, FORSCOM Mobilization and Deployment Planning System (FORMDEPS), FORSCOM Regulation 500-3-3, Volume III, Reserve Component Unit Commander's Handbook, Fort McPherson, Georgia, 15 July 1999: 27, 33.

language addresses the possibility of a false claim of same-sex behavior being used as a means of avoiding a mobilization. If such a claim is made, an investigation is likely to occur. If the claim is false, the individual would be retained (and possibly disciplined for making a false claim). If the claim is found to be true, a discharge would be in order. Retaining individuals who violate the rules pertaining to gays, lesbians or bisexuals in uniform is a violation of federal law.

Listed in Table 1 are the homosexual discharge statistics from FY1980 to FY2009. In January 1981, the then-current policy on administrative discharges for homosexuality was reinstituted under new wording to allow for the continuation of homosexual discharges while addressing legal concerns over the wording of the previous policy.[38] The active duty force numbered approximately 2.1 million throughout the 1980s. By FY2000, active duty personnel numbers fell to a then low of 1,384,338. The numbers increased to 1,434,377 in FY2004 and seemed to level off and then decline thereafter. Because of this drop in manpower levels, it is important to consider not just the number of homosexual discharges in any particular year, but the changes in discharges as a percentage of the total active force.

The data in Table 1 show the percentage of discharges fell from FY1982 to FY1994. The percentage of discharges rose from FY1 994 to FY2001. In FY2001, the number/percentage discharged was smaller than the previous peak of FY1982.

Table 1. Homosexual Conduct Administrative Separation Discharge Statistics

Fiscal Year	Total Number of Homosexual Discharges	Percentage of Total Active Force
1980	1,754	0.086
1981	1,817	0.088
1982	1,998	0.095
1983	1,815	0.085
1984	1,822	0.085
1985	1,660	0.077
1986	1,643	0.076
1987	1,380	0.063
1988	1,101	0.051
1989	996	0.047

[38] See Burrelli, David F., "An Overview of the Debate on Homosexuals in the U.S. Military," in *Gays and Lesbians in the Military, Issues, Concerns, and Contrasts,* Scott, Wilbur J., and Sandra Carson Stanley, eds., Aldine de Gruyter, New York, 1994: 18-19.

Fiscal Year	Total Number of Homosexual Discharges	Percentage of Total Active Force
1990	941	0.046
1991	949	0.048
1992	730	0.040
1993	682	0.040
1994	617	0.038
1995	757	0.050
1996	858	0.058
1997	997	0.069
1998	1,145	0.081
1999	1,034	0.075
2000	1,212	0.088
2001	1,227	0.089
2002	885	0.063
2003	770	0.054
2004	653	0.046
2005	726	0.052
2006	612	0.044
2007	635	0.046
2008	634	0.045
2009	428	0.030

Sources: Data for the years 1980 through 1997 are from U.S. Department of Defense, Office of the Assistant Secretary of Defense (Personnel and Readiness), Report to the Secretary of Defense, *Review of the Effectiveness of the Application and Enforcement of the Department's Policy on Homosexual Conduct in the Military*, April 1998. Percentages may vary slightly due to rounding. Data for later years are from the Department of Defense, Defense Manpower Data Center. Year 2005 data are from Files, John, "Military's discharges for being gay rose in '05," *New York Times*, August 15, 2006. Data from 2006-2009 are from DOD office of Legislative Affairs.

Since FY2001, the numbers/percentages have begun to decline and later level off. These percentages were declining prior to, and continued to decline following the 1991 Persian Gulf War (Operations Desert Shield/Desert Storm). If, as some have speculated, DOD was using "Stop Loss" to retain gays, lesbians and bisexuals during that war, one would expect to see a drop in the wartime discharge rate followed by an increase following the crisis. Such a pattern is not evident in these data.

During the period covered by these data, the average percentage discharged was 0.063%. For the period prior to the implementation of the "Don't Ask, Don't Tell" policy (and the "Don't Tell" law), i.e., FY1980 to FY1992, the average percentage discharged was 0.068%. For the period FY1993 to FY2009, the average was 0.057%. The difference in the percentage discharged before and following the implementation of this policy was statistically insignificant. Thus, although the data appear to move in differing directions prior to and following the implementation of the new policy, statistical analysis suggests that such changes may reflect random fluctuations in the data.[39]

RECENT LEGISLATION

H.R. 1283, the Military Readiness Enhancement Act of 2009 would repeal current Department of Defense (DOD) policy concerning homosexuality in the Armed Forces. It would prohibit the Secretary of Defense and the Secretary of Homeland Security with respect to the Coast Guard when it is not operating as a service in the Navy, from discriminating on the basis of sexual orientation against any member of the Armed Forces or any person seeking to become a member. Further, the act would authorize the re-accession into the Armed Forces of otherwise qualified individuals previously separated for homosexuality, bisexuality, or homosexual conduct.

Finally, the act would require such Secretaries to ensure that regulations governing the personal conduct of members of the Armed Forces are written and enforced without regard to sexual orientation.[40]

S. 3065, the Military Readiness Enhancement Act of 2010, would repeal current Department of Defense (DOD) policy concerning homosexuality in the Armed Forces. It would prohibit the Secretary of Defense and the Secretary of Homeland Security with respect to the Coast Guard when it is not operating as a service in the Navy, from discriminating on the basis of sexual orientation against any member of the Armed Forces or any person seeking to become a member. Further, the act would authorize the re-accession into the Armed Forces of otherwise qualified individuals previously separated for homosexuality, bisexuality, or homosexual conduct.

[39] Student's "t test," introduced by W.S. Gossett, under the pseudonym "Student," is used in this instance to measure differences of means between two sets of data taking into consideration the dispersion of data in each set and the number of cases involved in each set as well. These differences in means are considered in terms of their relative probability compared to random sampling distributions of samples of the same size. If the differences are small, as was the case here, the explanation that any difference is due to random factors in the data can not be rejected. In other words, the data do not support a conclusion that the change in policy had a statistical effect on discharge rates. See Blalock, Hubert M., Jr., Social Statistics, 2nd ed., New York: McGraw-Hill, 1972: 220-241. For these data, $t=1.6479$, prob. > 0.05, with 28 degrees of freedom, with equal variances.

[40] Reprinted from the Legislative Information Service of the U.S. Congress, August 12, 2009.

Finally, the act would require such Secretaries to ensure that regulations governing the personal conduct of members of the Armed Forces are written and enforced without regard to sexual orientation.[41]

APPENDIX. 10 USC §654

10 United States Code §654. Policy Concerning Homosexuality in the Armed Forces

(a) Findings.—Congress makes the following findings:

(1) Section 8 of article I of the Constitution of the United States commits exclusively to the Congress the powers to raise and support armies, provide and maintain a Navy, and make rules for the government and regulation of the land and naval forces.

(2) There is no constitutional right to serve in the armed forces.

(3) Pursuant to the powers conferred by section 8 of article I of the Constitution of the United States, it lies within the discretion of the Congress to establish qualifications for and conditions of service in the armed forces.

(4) The primary purpose of the armed forces is to prepare for and to prevail in combat should the need arise.

(5) The conduct of military operations requires members of the armed forces to make extraordinary sacrifices, including the ultimate sacrifice, in order to provide for the common defense.

(6) Success in combat requires military units that are characterized by high morale, good order and discipline, and unit cohesion.

(7) One of the most critical elements in combat capability is unit cohesion, that is, the bonds of trust among individual service members that make the combat effectiveness of a military unit greater than the sum of the combat effectiveness of the individual unit members.

(8) Military life is fundamentally different from civilian life in that—

(A) the extraordinary responsibilities of the armed forces, the unique conditions of military service, and the critical role of unit cohesion, require that the military community, while subject to civilian control, exist as a specialized society; and

[41] Reprinted from H.R. 1283, see body of the text for further discussion.

(B) the military society is characterized by its own laws, rules, customs, and traditions, including numerous restrictions on personal behavior, that would not be acceptable in civilian society.

(9) The standards of conduct for members of the armed forces regulate a member's life for 24 hours each day beginning at the moment the member enters military status and not ending until that person is discharged or otherwise separated from the armed forces.

(10)Those standards of conduct, including the Uniform Code of Military Justice, apply to a member of the armed forces at all times that the member has a military status, whether the member is on base or off base, and whether the member is on duty or off duty.

(11)The pervasive application of the standards of conduct is necessary because members of the armed forces must be ready at all times for worldwide deployment to a combat environment.

(12)The worldwide deployment of United States military forces, the international responsibilities of the United States, and the potential for involvement of the armed forces in actual combat routinely make it necessary for members of the armed forces involuntarily to accept living conditions and working conditions that are often spartan, primitive, and characterized by forced intimacy with little or no privacy.

(13)The prohibition against homosexual conduct is a longstanding element of military law that continues to be necessary in the unique circumstances of military service.

(14)The armed forces must maintain personnel policies that exclude persons whose presence in the armed forces would create an unacceptable risk to the armed forces' high standards of morale, good order and discipline, and unit cohesion that are the essence of military capability.

(15)The presence in the armed forces of persons who demonstrate a propensity or intent to engage in homosexual acts would create an unacceptable risk to the high standards of morale, good order and discipline, and unit cohesion that are the essence of military capability.

(b) Policy.—A member of the armed forces shall be separated from the armed forces under regulations prescribed by the Secretary of Defense if one or more of the following findings is made and approved in accordance with procedures set forth in such regulations:

(1) That the member has engaged in, attempted to engage in, or solicited another to engage in a homosexual act or acts unless there are further findings, made and approved in accordance with procedures set forth in such regulations, that the member has demonstrated that—
 (A) such conduct is a departure from the member's usual and customary behavior;
 (B) such conduct, under all the circumstances, is unlikely to recur;
 (C) such conduct was not accomplished by use of force, coercion, or intimidation;
 (D) under the particular circumstances of the case, the member's continued presence in the armed forces is consistent with the interests of the armed forces in proper discipline, good order, and morale; and
 (e) the member does not have a propensity or intent to engage in homosexual acts.

(2) That the member has stated that he or she is a homosexual or bisexual, or words to that effect, unless there is a further finding, made and approved in accordance with procedures set forth in the regulations, that the member has demonstrated that he or she is not a person who engages in, attempts to engage in, has a propensity to engage in, or intends to engage in homosexual acts.

(3) That the member has married or attempted to marry a person known to be of the same biological sex.

(c) Entry Standards and Documents.—
 (1) The Secretary of Defense shall ensure that the standards for enlistment and appointment of members of the armed forces reflect the policies set forth in subsection (b).
 (2) The documents used to effectuate the enlistment or appointment of a person as a member of the armed forces shall set forth the provisions of subsection (b).

(d) Required Briefings.—The briefings that members of the armed forces receive upon entry into the armed forces and periodically thereafter under section 937 of this title (article 137 of the Uniform Code of Military Justice) shall include a detailed explanation of the applicable laws and regulations governing sexual conduct by members of the armed forces, including the policies prescribed under subsection (b).

(e) Rule of Construction.—Nothing in subsection (b) shall be construed to require that a member of the armed forces be processed for separation from the armed forces when a determination is made in accordance with regulations prescribed by the Secretary of Defense that—

(1) the member engaged in conduct or made statements for the purpose of avoiding or terminating military service; and

(2) separation of the member would not be in the best interest of the armed forces.

(f) Definitions.—In this section:

(1) The term "homosexual" means a person, regardless of sex, who engages in, attempts to engage in, has a propensity to engage in, or intends to engage in homosexual acts, and includes the terms "gay" and "lesbian".

(2) The term "bisexual" means a person who engages in, attempts to engage in, has a propensity to engage in, or intends to engage in homosexual and heterosexual acts.

(3) The term "homosexual act" means—

(A) any bodily contact, actively undertaken or passively permitted, between members of the same sex for the purpose of satisfying sexual desires; and

(B) any bodily contact which a reasonable person would understand to demonstrate a propensity or intent to engage in an act described in subparagraph (A).

In: New Developments in Human Rights
Editors: J. M. Bauer and C. P. Davies
ISBN 978-1-61324-316-9

Chapter 5

VIOLENCE AGAINST WOMEN ACT: HISTORY AND FEDERAL FUNDING

Garrine P. Laney*
Social Policy

SUMMARY

The Violence Against Women and Department of Justice Reauthorization Act of 2005 (VAWA 2005) (P.L. 109-162) was enacted on January 5, 2006. Among other things, VAWA 2005 reauthorized existing VAWA programs and created many new programs. The act encourages collaboration among law enforcement, judicial personnel, and public and private service providers to victims of domestic and sexual violence; increases public awareness of domestic violence; addresses the special needs of victims of domestic and sexual violence, including the elderly, disabled, children, youth, and individuals of ethnic and racial communities; authorizes long-term and transitional housing for victims; makes some provisions gender-neutral; and requires studies and reports on the effectiveness of approaches used for certain grants in combating violence.

VAWA programs are funded through annual appropriations for both the Departments of Justice (DOJ) and Health and Human Services (HHS). President Barack Obama released his FY2011 budget on February 2, 2011, requesting funding of $649.36 million for violence against women programs. For programs

* Email: glaney@crs.loc.gov

administered by DOJ, the President requests $457.00 million, of which $187.50 million is for Services-Training-Officers-Prosecutors (STOP) formula grants and $25.00 million is for Transitional Housing Assistance grants. The FY20 11 funding request for programs administered by HHS is $192.36 million, of which $140.00 million is for Family Violence Prevention/Grants for Battered Women's Shelters and $5.00 million is for the National Domestic Violence Hotline.

The Obama Administration requests FY20 11 funding of $500,000 each for two new efforts to address sexual and domestic violence and stalking in Indian Country: (1) Indian Country—Sexual Assault Clearinghouse and (2) Indian Country—Regional Summits.

On December 16, 2009, the Consolidated Appropriations Act, 2010 (P.L. 111-117; H.R. 3288) was enacted, providing total FY20 10 funding of $625.91 million for violence against women programs, of which $444.50 million is for VAWA programs administered by DOJ and $181.41 million is for domestic violence programs under the Department of Health and Human Services.

The original VAWA, enacted in 1994 as Title IV of the Violent Crime Control and Law Enforcement Act (P.L. 103-322), established within DOJ and HHS formula and discretionary grant programs for state, local, and Indian tribal governments. The Violence Against Women Act of 2000 (VAWA 2000; P.L. 106-386), reauthorized many VAWA programs, set new funding levels, and created new grant programs to address sexual assaults on campuses and assist victims of domestic abuse. The Keeping Children and Families Safe Act of 2003 (P.L. 108-36) and the PROTECT Act (P.L. 108-2 1) authorized funding of both HHS and DOJ transitional housing assistance programs for victims of domestic violence. This report will be updated to reflect legislative activity.

Recent Developments

President Barack Obama's FY20 11 budget request is $649.36 million for violence against women programs, of which $457.00 million is for programs administered by the Department of Justice (DOJ) and $192.36 million is for programs administered by the Department of Health and Human Services (HHS). (For further details on the funding of violence against women programs, see the section later in this report on "Funding for Violence Against Women Programs.")

On December 16, 2009, the President signed into law the Consolidated Appropriations Act, 2010 (P.L. 111-117; H.R. 3288), providing total FY2010 funding of $625.91 million for violence against women programs, of which $444.50 million is for VAWA programs administered by DOJ and $181.41

million is for domestic violence programs under the Department of Health and Human Services. The act provides $210.00 million for the STOP grant program and $130.05 million for family violence/battered women's shelters.

HISTORY OF THE VIOLENCE AGAINST WOMEN ACT

While violence against women was identified as a serious problem in the 1 970s, legislation proposing a federal response to such violence was first introduced in the 1980s. Congressional action to address gender-related violence culminated in the enactment of two major laws—The Family Violence Prevention and Services Act[1] (FVPSA) and the Violence Against Women Act (VAWA), which is Title IV of the Violent Crime Control and Law Enforcement Act of 1994.[2] While appropriations for programs of both of these acts are included in this report, the focus of the discussion is VAWA.

The Family Violence Prevention Services Act

Enacted in 1984, the FVPSA assists states in preventing incidents of family violence and provides shelter and related assistance to victims of family violence and their dependents. The act authorizes programs that provide technical assistance and training on family violence to states, local public agencies, nonprofit private organizations, and others.[3]

Violence against Women Act

The Violence Against Women Act, originally enacted in 1994 as Title IV of the Violent Crime Control and Law Enforcement Act of 1994 (P.L. 103-322), emphasizes funding of enforcement efforts as well as educational and social programs to prevent crime. The focus of the funding is on local government programs, an approach that the sponsors of the legislation believed was the most promising technique for reducing crime and violence. The largest funded VAWA

[1] P.L. 98-457; 42 U.S.C. § 10401

[2] P.L. 103-322; 42 U.S.C. § 13701

[3] For a fuller discussion of the Family Violence Prevention and Services Act, see CRS Report R40473, *Family Violence Prevention and Services Act: Programs and Funding*, by Garrine P. Laney.

program, the Services-Training-Officers-Prosecutors (STOP) formula grants, is to help state governments, Indian tribal governments, and units of local government strengthen law enforcement, prosecution, and victims' services in cases involving violent crimes against women. These STOP grants may be used to provide personnel, training, technical assistance, data collection, and other equipment to increase the apprehension, prosecution, and adjudication of persons committing violent crimes against women.

VAWA funding for FY1995 through FY2000 was authorized through the Violent Crime Reduction Trust Fund (VCRTF), created under Title XXXI of P.L. 103-322. Authorization for VCRTF expired at the end of FY2000. Nonetheless, most of the programs in VAWA received appropriations for FY200 1.[4]

On October 28, 2000, President William J. Clinton signed into law the Victims of Trafficking and Violence Protection Act of 2000 (P.L. 106-386), of which Division B is the Violence Against Women Act of 2000 (VAWA 2000). The Violence Against Women Act of 2000 continued to support VAWA by reauthorizing existing programs and adding initiatives, including grants to assist victims of dating violence, transitional housing for victims of violence, a pilot program aimed at protecting children during visits with a parent who has been accused of domestic violence, and protections from violence for elderly and disabled women. It also made technical amendments, and required grant recipients to submit reports on the effectiveness of programs funded by the grants to aid with the dissemination of information on successful programs. The legislation amended the Public Health Service Act (P.L. 98-457) to require that certain funds be used exclusively for rape prevention and education programs. Moreover, the bill made it easier for a battered immigrant woman to leave the abuser and to help prosecute him. Under the old law, battered immigrant women could be deported if they left abusers who are their sponsors for residency and citizenship in the United States. VAWA 2000 created special rules for alien battered spouses and children to allow them to remain in the United States.[5]

---

[4] For detailed information on the grant programs, the application process, and grant programs in each state, please consult the Department of Justice's Office on Violence Against Women, at http://www.usdoj. gov/ovw/ ovwgrantprograms.htm.

[5] See RL3 0559, *Immigration: Noncitizen Victims of Family Violence*, by Andorra Bruno and Alison Siskin.

Changes in Federal Criminal Law

To help combat violence against women, the original VAWA rewrote several areas of federal criminal law. Penalties were created for interstate stalking or domestic abuse in cases where an abuser crossed a state line to injure or harass another, or forced a victim to cross a state line under duress and then physically harmed the victim in the course of a violent crime. Additionally, the law strengthened existing penalties for repeat sexual offenders and required restitution to victims in federal sex offense cases. VAWA called for pretrial detention in federal sex offense or child pornography felonies and allowed evidence of prior sex offenses to be used in some subsequent trials regarding federal sex crimes. The law also set new rules of evidence specifying that a victim's past sexual behavior generally was not admissible in federal civil or criminal cases regarding sexual misconduct.

Provisions of the original VAWA allowed rape victims to demand that their alleged assailants be tested for HIV, the virus that is generally believed to cause AIDS. A federal judge can order such a procedure after determining that risk to the victim existed.

As in the original Act, VAWA 2000 created new stalking offenses, changing the law to create penalties for a person who travels in interstate or foreign commerce with the intent to kill, injure, harass, or intimidate a spouse or intimate partner, and who in the course of such travel commits or attempts to commit a crime of violence against the spouse or intimate partner. It also created penalties for a person who causes a spouse or intimate partner to travel in interstate or foreign commerce by force or coercion and in the course of such travel commits or attempts to commit a crime of violence against the spouse or intimate partner.

The bill added the intimate partners of the victim as people covered under the interstate stalking statute, and made it a crime to use the mail or any facility of interstate or foreign commerce to engage in a course of conduct that would place a person in reasonable fear of harm to themselves or their immediate family or intimate partner.

Additionally, VAWA 2000 created penalties for any person who travels in interstate or foreign commerce with the intent of violating a protection order or causes a person to travel in interstate or foreign commerce by force or coercion and violates a protection order.[6]

[6] P.L. 106-386, Section 1107.

REAUTHORIZATION OF VAWA IN THE 109TH CONGRESS[7]

On January 5, 2006, President George W. Bush signed into law the Violence Against Women and Department of Justice Reauthorization Act of 2005 (VAWA 2005, P.L. 109-162).

VAWA 2005 reauthorizes many existing programs for FY2007 through FY2011, and authorizes a number of new programs for victims of domestic and dating violence, sexual assault, and stalking.

The act emphasizes collaboration among law enforcement, health and housing professionals, and women, men, and youth alliances, and encourages community initiatives to address these issues.

New programs seek to focus on young victims of violence; improve the health care system's response to violence; inform the public and employers about domestic and dating violence, sexual assault, and stalking; protect the privacy of victims of violence; provide housing assistance, including public housing, for battered women and children; and support outreach efforts to underserved populations such as ethnic, immigrant, and racial populations. In an effort to more closely monitor the status and performance of some of these programs, VAWA 2005 provides for some grant recipients to submit reports on policies and procedures they followed.

The act also provides funding for studies and research on effective interventions that prevent both acts and effects of domestic and dating violence, sexual assault, and stalking.

FUNDING FOR VIOLENCE AGAINST WOMEN PROGRAMS

FY2011

President Obama's FY2011 budget request for violence against women programs is $649.36 million, of which $457.00 million is for programs administered by DOJ and $192.36 million is for programs administered by HHS. The President requests $187.50 million for the DOJ STOP grant program,

[7] Provisions of VAWA legislation related to immigrant victims of violence (Title VIII) are not addressed in this report. For information on these provisions, contact Andorra Bruno (7-7865) or Alison Siskin (7-0260). In addition, Title XI of the legislation is the Department of Justice Reauthorization Act; see CRS Report RL33 111, *Department of Justice Reauthorization: Provisions to Improve Program Management, Compliance, and Evaluation of Justice Assistance Grants*, by Nathan James.

compared to FY2010 appropriations of $210.00 million. This is a net decrease for STOP grants of $1.50 million, when one considers that in FY2010 both the transitional housing assistance program and the National Institute for Justice (NIJ) were funded as set-asides under the STOP grant program at $18.00 million and $3.00 million, respectively. For FY2011 funding, the President requests separate line-items of $25.00 million for DOJ's transitional housing assistance program and $3.00 million for NIJ to conduct research on violence against Indian women.

For programs administered by HHS, the budget request is $130.05 million for the Family Violence Prevention/Battered Women's Shelters program, compared to FY20 10 appropriations of $127.78 million for the program. For the National Domestic Violence Hotline, the FY20 11 request is $3.21 million, a slight increase above the FY20 10 funding level. (See Table 2 for FY20 11 budget requests for violence against women programs.)

The President requests FY20 11 funding of $500,000 each for two new efforts to address sexual and domestic violence in Indian Country: (1) Indian Country—Sexual Assault Clearinghouse and (2) Indian Country—Regional Summits.

The Sexual Assault Clearinghouse is created to offer a one-stop shop where tribes, at their request, could receive free onsite training and technical assistance, which would enable the community to respond to events, treat victims, and promote awareness of sexual assault.

The Administration expects that eventually the clearinghouse would track emerging trends in the field and assist in developing a global perspective on sexual assault in Indian country. The regional summits would provide training on prosecuting federal cases of sexual and domestic violence and stalking in Indian country and improve collaboration among those federal and tribal entities that are charged with enhancing the safety of Indian women.

FY2010

On December 16, 2009, the Consolidated Appropriations Act, 2010 (P.L. 111-117; H.R. 3288) was enacted, providing total FY20 10 funding of $625.91 million for violence against women programs, of which $444.50 million is for VAWA programs administered by DOJ. Appropriations for the DOJ STOP grant program are $210.00 million. For domestic violence programs under the Department of Health and Human Services, the act provides $181.41 million in funding, as follows: $3.21 million for the National Domestic Violence Hotline, $130.05 million for the Battered Women's Shelters program, $42.62 million for

Rape Prevention programs, and $5.53 million for Community Initiative programs on Domestic Violence. (See Table 1.)

Actual appropriations for violence against women programs have tended to be less than the amounts authorized in the law. For each of FY2007 through FY20 10, the authorized funding level for violence against women programs is as follows: $1,005.00 million for FY2007, $1,003.00 million for FY2008, $793.50 million for FY2009, and $793.50 million for FY2010.

FY2009

On March 11, 2009, the Omnibus Appropriations Act for FY2009 (P.L. 111-8) was enacted, providing a total of $595.31 million for violence against women programs, of which $415.00 million and $180.31 million were for programs administered by DOJ and HHS, respectively. For DOJ administered programs, the act provided $190.00 million for STOP grants, which included set-asides of $18.00 million for transitional housing assistance, $1.88 million for the National Institute of Justice, and $0.40 million for the Native Alaskan Liaison Office. For HHS programs, the act provided $128.00 million for Grants for Battered Women's Shelters and $3.00 million for the National Domestic Violence Hotline programs.

For FY2009 (as for FY2008, see below), President George W. Bush proposed to consolidate formula and discretionary VAWA programs administered by the Office on Violence Against Women (OVW) and certain victims of child abuse programs that are currently administered by the Office of Justice Programs (OJP). The Administration stated that by consolidating VAWA programs in this way, it would eliminate formulas and earmarks and create one flexible, competitive discretionary grant program, called the Prevention and Prosecution of Violence Against Women and Related Victim Services Program. In addition, the Bush Administration stated that through a single application, grantees would be able to request funding for any of the current programs, which would be listed as eligible purposes under this new consolidated program. President Bush requested $280.00 million for this consolidated program. Senate Appropriations Committee report language rejected the President's proposal to consolidate VAWA programs, stating that it ignored congressional intent to meet the needs of youth, native women, communities of color, and victims of sexual violence, and to encourage collaborations among these distinct groups in addressing various aspects of domestic and sexual violence, and thereby strengthen intervention and prevention responses to victims, families, and communities.

Table 1. Funding for Violence against Women Programs, FY2009-FY2010 ($ in millions)

Program and Administrative Agency	FY2009 Enacted	FY2010 Authorization	FY2010 Budget Request	FY2010 Enacted
STOP Grants Improvements (Sec. 101) (42 U.S.C. 3793(a)(18) (OVW)	$190.00[a]	$225.00	$190.00[a]	$21 0.00[b]
Transitional Housing Assistance Grants for Victims of Domestic Violence, Stalking, or Sex-ual Assault (Sec. 602) (42 U.S.C.13975) (OVW)	(18.00)[a]	40.00	(18.00)[a]	(18.00)[b]
National Institute of Justice (for Research and Evaluation of Violence Against Women)	(1 .88)[a]		(3.00)[a]	(3.00)[b]
Grants to Encourage Arrest Policies (Sec. 102) (42 U.S.C. 3793(a)(19) (OVW)	60.00	75.00	60.00	60.00
Legal Assistance for Victims Improvements (Sec. 103) (42 U.S.C. 3796gg-6) (OVW)	37.00	65.00	37.00	41.00
Court Training and Improvements to Respond to Victims of Violence (Sec. 105) (42 U.S.C. 14043) (OVW)	3.00	5.00	3.00	3.00
Privacy Protections for Victims of Domestic, Dating, and Sexual Violence, and Stalking (Sec. 107) (42 U.S.C. 14043b) (OVW)	0.00	5.00	0.00	0.00
Sex Offender Management (Probation and Parole Officers Training) (Sec. 1167) (42 U.S.C. 13941) (OJP)	3.50	5.00	3.50	3.50
National Stalker and Domestic Violence Reduction Grants (Stalking Databases) (Sec. 109) (42 U.S.C. 14032) (OVW)	3.00	3.00	3.00	3.00
Federal Victims Assistants (Sec. 110) 119 Stat. 2984 (USA)	0.00	1.00	0.00	0.00

Table 1 (Continued)

Program and Administrative Agency	FY2009 Enacted	FY2010 Authorization	FY2010 Budget Request	FY2010 Enacted
Grants for Law Enforcement Training (Sec. 111) (42 U.S.C. 1 4044f)[c]	0.00	10.00	0.00	0.00
Court Appointed Special Advocates for Victims of Child Abuse (Sec. 112) (42 U.S.C.13011) (OJP)	15.00	12.00	15.00	15.00
Grants for Outreach to Underserved Populations (Sec. 120) (42 U.S.C. 14045) (OVW)	0.00	2.00	0.00	0.00
Sexual Assault Services Program (Sec. 202) (42 U.S.C. 3796gg-9) (OJP)	12.00	50.00	12.00	15.00
Rural Domestic Violence and Child Abuse En-forcement (Sec. 203) (42 U.S.C. 13971) (OVW)	41.00	55.00	41.00	41.00
Grants to Decrease Violence Against Women with Disabilities (Sec. 204) (42 U.S.C. 3796gg-7) (OVW)	6.75	10.00	6.75	6.75
Training and Services to End Violence Against and Abuse of Women Later in Life (Sec. 205) (42 U.S.C. 14041 a) (OVW)	4.25	10.00	4.25	4.25
Services to Advocate For and Respond to Youth Victims of Violence (Sec. 303) (42 U.S.C. 14043c) (OVW)	3.50	15.00	3.50	3.50
Access to Justice for Youth (Sec. 303) (42 U.S.C. 1 4043c- 1) (OVW)	0.00	5.00	0.00	0.00
Combating Domestic, Dating, and Sexual Violence, and Stalking in Middle and High Schools (STEP) (Sec. 303) (42 U.S.C. 1 4043c-3) (OVW)	0.00	5.00	0.00	2.50

Program and Administrative Agency	FY2009 Enacted	FY2010 Authorization	FY2010 Budget Request	FY2010 Enacted
Grants to Combat Violent Crimes on Campus (Sec. 304) (42 U.S.C. 14045b) (OVW)	9.50	15.00	9.50	9.50
Safe Havens for Children Pilot Program (Sec. 306) (42 U.S.C. 10420) (OVW)	14.00	20.00	14.00	14.00
Grants to Assist Children and Youth Exposed to Violence (Sec. 401) (42 U.S.C.14043d-2) (OVW)	3.00	20.00	3.00	3.00
Development of Curricula and Pilot Programs for Home Visitation Projects (Sec. 401) (42 U.S.C. 14043d-3) (OVW)	0.00	7.00	0.00	0.00
Engaging Men and Youth in Preventing Dom-estic, Dating, and Sexual Violence, and Stalking (Sec. 401) (42 U.S.C. 14043d-4) (OVW)	3.00	10.00	3.00	3.00
Public Awareness Campaign (Sec. 403) (42 U.S.C. 1 4045c) (OVW)	0.00	[d]	0.00	0.00
Grants to Combat Violence Against Women in Public and Assisted Housing (Sec. 601) (42 U.S.C. 1 4043e-4) (OVW)	0.00	10.00	0.00	0.00
Grants for National Resource Center on Workplace Responses to Assist Victims of Domestic and Sexual Violence (Sec. 701) (42 U.S.C. 14043f) (OVW)	1.00	1.00	1.00	1.00
Analysis and Research on Violence Against Indian Women Baseline Study (Sec. 904(a)) (42 U.S.C. 3796gg-10 note) (NIJ)	1.00	1.00	1.00	1.00
Tracking of Violence Against Indian Women—Access to Federal Criminal Information Databases (Sec. 905a) (OVW) / National Tribal Sex Offender Registry (Sec. 905b) (OJP)(28 U.S.C. 534(a))	1.00	1.00e	1.00	1.00

Table 1 (Continued)

Program and Administrative Agency	FY2009 Enacted	FY2010 Authorization	FY2010 Budget Request	FY2010 Enacted
Training for Judicial Personnel and Practitioners for Victims of Child Abuse (42 U.S.C. 13024) (OJP)	2.50	0.00	2.50	2.50
Grants for Televised Testimony by Victims of Child Abuse (42 U.S.C. 3793(a) (OJP)	1.00	[f]	1.00	1.00
Subtotal: Department of Justice	$415.00	$683.00	$415.00	$444.50
Training and Collaboration on Intersection of Domestic Violence and Child Maltreatment (Sec. 303) (42 U.S.C. 1 4043c-2) (FYSB)	0.00	5.00	0.00	0.00
National Domestic Violence Hotline(Sec. 411) (ACF)[g]	3.00	[h]	3.21	3.21
Grants for Battered Women's Shelters (Sec. 406) (ACF)[g]	127.78	[i]	127.78	130.05
Transitional Housing for Victims of Domestic Violence (Sec. 414) (ACF)	0.00	[j]	0.00	0.00
Rape Prevention and Education Grants (Sec. 302) (CDC)	42.52	80.00	42.62	42.62
Community Initiative Programs on Domestic Violence (Sec. 413) (CDC)	5.51	[k]	5.56	5.53
Prevention of Violence Study (Sec. 402) (42 U.S.C. 280b-4) (CDC)	0.00	2.00	0.00	0.00
Training and Education of Health Professionals on Domestic and Sexual Violence (Sec. 503) (42 U.S.C. 294h) (HRSA)	0.75	3.00	0.00	0.00
Grants to Foster Public Health Responses to Domestic, Dating, and Sexual Violence, and Stalking (Sec. 504) (42 U.S.C. 280g-4) (CDC)	0.75	5.00	0.00	0.00

Program and Administrative Agency	FY2009 Enacted	FY2010 Authorization	FY2010 Budget Request	FY2010 Enacted
Research on Effective Interventions in the Healthcare Setting (Sec. 505) (42 U.S.C. 13973) (CDC)	0.00	5.00	0.00	0.00
Collaborative Grants to Increase the Long-Term Stability of Victims (Sec. 601) (42 U.S.C. 1 4043e-3) (ACF)	0.00	10.00	0.00	0.00
Native Americans Injury Study (Sec. 904(b)) (IHS)	0.00	0.50	0.00	0.00
Subtotal: Department of Health and Human Services	$180.31	$110.50	179.18	$181.41
Grand Total	$595.31	$793.50	$594.17	$625.91

Sources: For FY20 10 budget request, see Budget of the United States Government: Appendix under named agencies. On December 16, 2009, the Consolidated Appropriations Act, 2010 was enacted (P.L. 111-117; H.R. 3288). The Omnibus Appropriations Act for FY2009 (P.L. 111-8), which includes appropriations for the Departments of Commerce, Justice and Education and Labor, Health and Human Services, and Education, became law on March 11, 2009. The American Recovery and Reinvestment Act (P.L. 111-5) became law on February 17, 2009. The Violence Against Women Act, 2005 (P.L. 109-162), became law on January 5, 2006.

Abbreviations: In DOJ: USA: United States Attorneys; OJP: Office of Justice Programs; OVW: Office on Violence Against Women; STEP: Supporting Teens Through Education and Protection Act. In HHS: ACF: Administration for Children and Families; CDC: Centers for Disease Control and Prevention; FYSB: Family and Youth Services Bureau; HRSA: Health, Resources and Services Administration; IHS: Indian Health Service.

Notes:

(1) For FY2009, the American Recovery and Reinvestment Act provides $225 million in funding for the Office on Violence Against Women, of which $175 million is for STOP grants and $50 million is for the transitional housing assistance for victims of domestic violence program.

(2) Section numbers refer to the Violence Against Women Act, P.L. 109-162, unless otherwise indicated. Totals may not add due to rounding.

a. The Omnibus Appropriations Act for FY2009 provided $190 million for STOP grants, which included set-asides of $1.88 million for the National Institute of Justice (NIJ), $18 million for the transitional housing assistance program, and $0.40 million for the Native Alaskan Liaison Office. For FY20 10, the President's budget request was $190 million for STOP grants, which included set-asides of $3 million for NIJ, $18 million for transitional housing assistance, and $10 million for the Safe Start program.

b. The Consolidated Appropriations Act, 2010 provides $210 million for STOP grants, which includes set-asides of $18 million for transitional housing assistance grants and $3 million for the National Institute of Justice for Research and Evaluation of Violence Against Women.
c. DOJ has yet to determine the administering office for this program.
d. VAWA 2005 authorized "such sums as may be necessary" for the Public Awareness Campaign.
e. VAWA 2005 authorizes total funding of $1 million for Section 905, Tracking of Violence Against Indian Women, which includes two programs—access to federal criminal information databases and the national tribal sex offender registry.
f. VAWA 2005 did not reauthorize this program.
g. This section number is from the Keeping Children and Families Safe Act (P.L. 108-36), which amends the Family Violence Prevention and Services Act.
h. Authorization for the National Domestic Violence Hotline expired in FY2008. Under provisions of the Keeping Children and Families Safe Act, the National Domestic Violence Hotline was reauthorized at $3.5 million for each of FY2004 through FY2008. The National Domestic Violence Hotline was originally authorized under the Family Violence Prevention and Services Act (FVPSA). Introduced on November 19, 2009, H.R. 4116, the FVPSA [Family Violence Prevention and Services Act] Reauthorization Act of 2009 would reauthorize this program for each of FY20 10 through FY20 14.
i. Authorization for the Grants for Battered Women's Shelters program expired in FY2008. Under provisions of the Keeping Children and Families Safe Act of 2003, the Grants for Battered Women's Shelters program was reauthorized at $175 million for each of FY2004 through FY2008. The FVPSA Reauthorization Act of 2009 would reauthorize this program for each of FY20 10 through FY20 14.
j. Authorization for Transitional Housing for Victims of Domestic Violence, administered by HHS, expired after FY2008. This HHS program never received appropriations.
k. Authorization for Community Initiative Programs on Domestic Violence expired after FY2008. The Keeping Children and Families Safe Act of 2003 reauthorized the Community Initiative Program at $6 million for each of FY2004 through FY2008. The FVPSA Reauthorization Act of 2009 would reauthorize this program for each of FY20 10 through FY20 14.

American Recovery and Reinvestment Act

Enacted on February 17, 2009, the American Recovery and Reinvestment Act (P.L. 111-5) provided additional FY2009 funding of $225.00 million for the Office on Violence Against Women, of which $175.00 million was for STOP grants and $50.00 million was for the transitional housing assistance program.

Table 2. FY2011 Authorizations and Budget Request for Violence against Women Programs (in millions)

Program and Administrative Agency	FY2011 Authorization	FY2011 Budget Request
STOP Grants Improvements (Sec. 101) (42 U.S.C. 3793(A)(18) OVW	$225.00	$187.50
Transitional Housing Assistance Grants for Victims of Domestic Violence, Stalking, or Sexual Assault (Sec.602) (42 U.S.C.13975) (OVW)	40.00	25.00
Grants To Encourage Arrest Policies (Sec. 102) (42 U.S.C. 3793(a)(19) (OVW)	75.00	47.50
Legal Assistance for Victims Improvements (Sec. 103) (42 U.S.C. 3796gg-6)(OVW)	65.00	50.00
Court Training and Improvements to Respond to Victims of Violence (Sec. 105) (42 U.S.C. 14043) (OVW)	5.00	4.00
Privacy Protections for Victims of Domestic, Dating, and Sexual Violence, and Stalking (Sec. 107) (42 U.S.C. 14043b) (OVW)	5.00	—[m]
Sex Offender Management (Probation and Parole Officers Training) (Sec. 1167) (42 U.S.C. 13941) (OJP)	5.00	3.50
National Stalker and Domestic Violence Reduction Grants (Stalking Databases) (Sec. 109) (42 U.S.C. 14032) (OVW)	3.00	3.00
Federal Victims Assistance (Sec. 110) 119 Stat. 2984 (USA)	1.00	—[m]
Grants for Law Enforcement Training (Sec. 111) (42 U.S.C. 140440)[a]	10.00	—[m]
Court Appointed Special Advocates for Victims of Child Abuse (Sec. 112) (42 U.S.C. 13011) (OJP)	12.00	10.00
Grants for Outreach to Underserved Populations (Sec. 120) (42 U.S.C. 14045) (OVW)	2.00	—[m]
Sexual Assault Services Program (Sec. 202) (42 U.S.C. 1 4043g) (OVW)	50.00	30.00
Rural Domestic Violence and Child Abuse Enforcement (Sec. 203) (42 U.S.C. 13971) (OVW)	55.00	41.00
Grants to Decrease Violence Against Women with Disabilities (Sec. 204) (42 U.S.C. 3796gg-7) (OVW)	10.00	6.75

Table 2 (Continued)

Program and Administrative Agency	FY2011 Authorization	FY2011 Budget Request
Training and Services to End Violence Against and Abuse of Women Later in Life (Sec. 205) (42 U.S.C. 14041a) (OVW)	10.00	4.25
Services to Advocate for and Respond to Youth Victims of Violence (Sec. 303) (42 U.S.C. 14043c) (OVW)	15.00	3.50
Access to Justice for Youth (Sec. 303) (42 U.S.C. 14043c-1) (OVW)	5.00	—[m]
Combating Domestic, Dating, and Sexual Violence, and Stalking in Middle and High Schools [STEP] (Sec. 304) (42 U.S.C. 14043c-3) (OVW)	5.00	—[m]
Grants to Combat Violent Crimes on Campus (Sec. 304) (42 U.S.C. 14045b) (OVW)	15.00	9.50
Safe Havens for Children Pilot Program (Sec. 306) (42 U.S.C. 10420) (OVW)	20.00	14.00
Grants to Assist Children and Youth Exposed to Violence (Sec. 401) (42 U.S.C. 14043d-2) (OVW)	20.00	3.00
Development of Curricula and Pilot Programs for Home Visitation Projects (Sec. 401) (42 U.S.C. 14043d-3) (OVW)	7.00	—[m]
Engaging Men and Youth in Preventing Domestic, Dating, and Sexual Violence, and Stalking (Sec. 401) (42 U.S.C. 14043d-4) (OVW)	10.00	3.00
Public Awareness Campaign	—[b]	—[m]
Grants to Combat Violence Against Women in Public and Assisted Housing (Sec. 601) (42 U.S.C. 14043e-4) (OVW)	10.00	—[m]
Grants for National Resource Center on Workplace Responses to Assist Victims of Domestic and Sexual Violence (Sec. 701) (42 U.S.C. 14043f) (OVW)	1.00	1.00
Analysis and Research on Violence Against Indian Women Baseline Study (Sec. 904(a)) (42 U.S.C. 3796gg-10 note) (NIJ)	—[c]	3.00
Tracking of Violence Against Indian Women—Access to Federal Criminal Information Databases (Sec. 905a) (OVW) / National Tribal Sex Offender Registry (Sec. 905b) (OJP) (28 U.S.C. 534(a))	1.00	1.00

Program and Administrative Agency	FY2011 Authorization	FY2011 Budget Request
Research and Evaluation of Violence Against Women (NIJ)	—[d]	3.00[d]
Training for Judicial Personnel and Practitioners for Victims of Child Abuse (42 U.S.C. 13024) (OJP)	—[e]	2.50
Grants for Televised Testimony by Victims of Child Abuse (42 U.S.C. 3793(a) (OJP)	—[f]	0.00[f]
Indian Country—Sexual Assault Clearinghouse	[g]	0.50
Indian Country—Regional Summits	[h]	0.50
Subtotal: Department of Justice	$677.00	$457.00
Grants for Training and Collaboration on Intersection of Domestic Violence and Child Maltreatment (Sec. 303) (42 U.S.C. 14043c-2) (FYSB)	5.00	—[i]
National Domestic Violence Hotline (Sec. 411) (ACF)	—[j]	5.00
Grants for Battered Women's Shelters (Sec. 406) (ACF)	—[k]	140.00
Rape Prevention and Education Grants (Sec. 302) (CDC)	80.00	41.93
Community Initiative Programs on Domestic Violence (Sec. 413) (CDC)	—[l]	5.43
Prevention of Violence Study (Sec. 402) (42 U.S.C. 280b-4) (CDC)	2.00	—[m]
Training and Education of Health Professionals on Domestic and Sexual Violence (Sec. 503) (42 U.S.C. 294h) (HRSA)	3.00	—[m]
Grants to Foster Public Health Responses to Domestic, Dating, and Sexual Violence, and Stalking (Sec. 504) (42 U.S.C. 280g-4) (CDC)	5.00	—[m]
Research on Effective Interventions in the Healthcare Setting (Sec. 505) (42 U.S.C. 13973) (CDC)	5.00	—[m]
Collaborative Grants to Increase the Long-Term Stability of Victims (Sec. 601) (42 U.S.C. 14043e-3) (ACF)	10.00	—[m]
Native Americans Injury Study (Sec. 904) (IHS)	—[n]	—[m]
Subtotal: Department of Health and Human Services	$110.00	$192.36
Totals	$787.00	$649.36

Sources: FY20 11 Budget Request Documents and the Violence Against Women Act, 2005 (P.L. 109-162).

Notes: Section numbers refer to the Violence Against Women Act, P.L. 109-162, unless otherwise indicated. Totals may not add due to rounding.

a. DOJ has yet to determine the administering office for this program.

b. VAWA 2005 authorized such sums as necessary only through FY20 10.

c. VAWA 2005 authorized this program at $1 million for each of FY2007 through FY2008.

d. There is no authorization in VAWA 2005 for this research; however, it was funded in FY20 10 as a set-aside of $3 million from the STOP grant program. For FY20 11, the President requests $3 million for this research as a separate line-item.

e. The authorization for training for Judicial Personnel expired at the end of FY2005. Congress, however, has continued to fund it. (The Victims of Trafficking and Violence Protection Act of 2000 had authorized this program for each of FY200 1 through FY2005.)

f. VAWA 2005 did not reauthorize Grants for Televised Testimony by Victims of Child Abuse. Congress, however, has continued to fund it. Grants for Televised Testimony is administered by DOJ's Office of Justice Programs. President Obama did not request FY20 11 funding for this grant program.

g. The Obama Administration's FY20 11 budget request creates this clearinghouse effort.

h. The Obama Administration's FY20 1 1 budget request creates the regional summits effort.

i. No separate line-item funding indicated.

j. Authorization for the National Domestic Violence Hotline expired in FY2008, but Congress has continued to fund it. Under provisions of the Keeping Children and Families Safe Act, the National Domestic Violence Hotline was reauthorized at $3.5 million for each of FY2004 through FY2008. The National Domestic Violence Hotline was originally authorized under the Family Violence Prevention and Services Act (FVPSA). Introduced on November 19, 2009, H.R. 4116, the FVPSA Reauthorization Act of 2009, would reauthorize this program for each of FY20 10 through FY20 14.

k. Authorization for the Grants for Battered Women's Shelters expired in FY2008, but Congress has continued to fund it. Under provisions of the Keeping Children and Families Safe Act, the Grants for Battered Women's Shelters was authorized at $175 million for each of FY2004 through FY2008. The Grants for Battered Women's Shelters was originally authorized under FVPSA. The FVPSA Reauthorization Act of 2009 (H.R. 4116) would reauthorize this program for each of FY20 10 through FY2014.

l. Authorization for the Community Initiatives program expired in FY2008, but Congress has continued to fund it. Under provisions of the Keeping Children and Families Safe Act, the Community Initiatives Program on Domestic Violence was authorized at $6 million for each of FY2004 through FY2008. The FVPSA Reauthorization Act of

2009 (H.R. 4116) would reauthorize the program for each of FY20 10 through FY20 14.

m. No line item was indicated in the FY20 11 budget.

n. VAWA 2005 authorized $500,000 to be appropriated for each of FY2007 and FY2008.

VAWA Historical Funding (Covering FY2001-FY2008)

FY2008

President George W. Bush signed the Consolidated Appropriations Act for FY2008 (P.L. 110-161) on December 26, 2007, which provided total funding of $572.47 million for violence against women programs administered by DOJ and HHS. As established by VAWA 2005, the FY2008 authorization level for VAWA programs and studies administered by the Department of Justice (DOJ) was $683.00 million; total FY2008 authorization for programs administered by HHS was $320.00 million.

The President's FY2008 total budget request for VAWA programs was $546.28 million ($370.00 million and $176.28 million for programs administered by DOJ and HHS, respectively). President Bush's FY2008 request included $2.97 million for the domestic violence hotline and $124.73 million for battered women's shelters, two programs administered by HHS. According to the Centers for Disease Control and Prevention (CDC), the President's FY2008 budget request also included funding for two violence against women initiatives that did not receive a specific line item in the Administration's budget.

DOJ Funding

The Consolidated Appropriations Act for FY2008 provided $400.00 million for VAWA programs administered by DOJ. The act provided funding for several newly authorized programs by VAWA 2005. Programs such as services for children and youth exposed to violence, engaging men and youth in preventing domestic, dating and sexual violence and stalking, and services to advocate for and respond to youth victims of violence received funding of $2.82 million each, while research relating to violence against Indian women and the national tribal sex offender registry received $0.94 million each. The court training and improvements to respond to victims of violence and the sexual assault services programs, which were not funded in FY2007, received FY2008 funding of $2.82 million and $9.40 million, respectively. For FY2008, funding for some programs decreased slightly, including grants to encourage arrest policies, legal assistance for victims improvements, and sex offender management.

Proposal to Consolidate VAWA Programs

In its FY2008 budget request, the DOJ proposed to consolidate VAWA programs administered by the Office on Violence Against Women (OVW) into one flexible, competitive discretionary grant program, including three programs (Stalking Databases, Comprehensive Approaches to Sexual Offender Management, and Sexual Assault Services) that are currently administered by the Office of Justice Programs. In the DOJ budget justification language and on March 29, 2007 at a hearing of the House Appropriations Subcommittee on Commerce-Justice-Science, DOJ stated that its consolidation proposal would reduce the time grantees spent in applying for grants, eliminate earmarks and formulas, and allow multiple domestic violence and sexual assault needs to be addressed and dictated based on local conditions.

Both the House and Senate Appropriations Committees, however, rejected this proposal. Senate report language (S. 1745; S.Rept. 110-124) stated that VAWA programs are designed to meet specific needs and to support collaboration among distinct groups to enable them to use their expertise and resources in addressing different aspects of domestic and sexual violence. These VAWA programs have many specific requirements and protections to ensure that a collaborative effort with law enforcement, child protective services, health care, etc. is effective and remains confidential, and that the safety of victims is maintained. According to the Senate Appropriations Committee report, under the DOJ proposal, programs would have ceased to operate as Congress intended, would have been less successful, and could have disadvantaged certain applicants for VAWA funds, such as those in rural areas.

HHS Funding

The Consolidated Appropriations Act for FY2008 provided for a spending cut of 1.747% for programs funded in the Labor-HHS-Education division of the act. Funding of $172.47 million for violence against women programs administered by HHS reflects this spending cut. For FY2008, the battered women's shelters program received $122.55 million, while the national domestic violence hotline received $2.92 million. FY2008 funding levels for these two program were slightly below the FY2007 appropriations. Two programs administered by the Centers for Disease Control and Prevention—the rape prevention and education grant and community initiative programs on domestic violence—were funded at $42.00 million and $5.00 million, respectively.

FY2007

Total FY2007 funding of $558.92 million for VAWA programs was provided by the Revised Continuing Appropriations Resolution (P.L. 110-5), which was enacted on February 15, 2007. This resolution provided FY2007 appropriations of $382.57 million for violence against women programs administered by DOJ and $176.35 million for programs administered by HHS, of which $124.73 million was for battered women's shelters and $2.97 million was for the domestic violence hotline.

For FY2007, President George W. Bush requested $543.32 million for violence against women programs, of which $366.12 million and $177.20 million was for programs administered by DOJ and HHS, respectively. The Administration requested $172.99 million for STOP grants, of which $2.48 million was for the National Institute of Justice for research and evaluation of violence against women and $14.86 million was for transitional housing assistance grants; the President did not request funding for the Safe Start Program (Office of Juvenile Justice and Delinquency Prevention) which was authorized at $10.00 million. The President's request for HHSadministered programs included $125.00 million for battered women's shelters and $3.00 million for the domestic violence hotline.

FY2006

Total FY2006 appropriations for violence against women programs were $564.57 million, of which $388.07 million was for programs administered by DOJ and $176.50 million was for programs administered by HHS. (Total amounts for programs administered by both DOJ and HHS reflected the across-the-board rescission reductions of 1% for FY2006 discretionary appropriations.)

For FY2006, President George W. Bush requested a total of $515.00 million for violence against women programs, of which $386.00 million was for programs administered by DOJ and $129.00 million was for programs administered by HHS. On November 22, 2005, President Bush signed the Departments of State, Justice, and Commerce, and Related Agencies Appropriations Act, FY2006 (P.L. 109-108; H.R. 2862). FY2006 funding for STOP grants was $184.91 million. Transitional housing assistance was funded as a set-aside from STOP grants as in FY2005; however, the amount of the FY2006 set-aside was $15.00 million, compared with the FY2005 set-aside of $12.30 million. Some other violence against women programs also received small increases in funding for FY2006.

On December 30, 2005, the Departments of Labor, Health and Human Services, and Education, and Related Agencies Appropriations Act, 2006 (Labor-HHS-Ed Act) was enacted (P.L. 109-149, H.R. 3010). The Labor HHS-Ed

Act provided total FY2006 appropriations of $176.50 million for violence against women programs, including $124.73 million for the family violence/battered women's shelters program and $2.97 million for the national domestic violence hotline.

FY2005

On December 8, 2004, the Consolidated Appropriations Act, 2005 (P.L. 108-447) was enacted. The act provided $384.20 million in FY2005 funding for violence against women programs administered by DOJ. This amount included $185.00 million for the STOP grant program, of which $12.30 million was for transitional housing assistance grants for victims of domestic violence, stalking, or sexual assault. The act provided $179.50 million for programs administered by HHS, of which $126.65 million was for the battered women's shelters program and $3.25 million was for the national domestic violence hotline. Total FY2005 funding for violence against women programs administered by DOJ and HHS was $563.70 million. The Consolidated Appropriations Act, 2005 mandated a funding reduction of 0.80% for some FY2005 discretionary appropriations, which included VAWA funding. In addition, there was a 0.54% cut in Commerce-Justice-State discretionary appropriations for FY2005 that affected funding for violence against women programs administered by DOJ. Total authorized funding for violence against women programs for FY2002 was $626.80 million.

For FY2005, President George W. Bush requested a total of $514.11 million for violence against women programs, compared to FY2005 authorization levels of $729.00 million. Of the requested funding, $385.50 million was for grants administered by the DOJ and $128.65 million was for programs administered by HHS. These violence against women programs addressed domestic violence and improved services for victims and their dependents. The Bush Administration requested $15.00 million for the transitional housing assistance programs as a set-aside under the VAWA STOP Formula Grant Program.

FY2004

The Consolidated Appropriations Act for FY2004 became law on January 23, 2004 (P.L. 108-199; H.R. 2673). Congress appropriated total FY2004 funding of $517.00 million for violence against women programs. This compared to President Bush's total request of $512.40 million for violence against women grant programs. For violence against women programs that were administered by DOJ, Congress provided $387.60 million. For domestic violence programs that were administered by HHS, the conference agreement provided $129.40 million, of which $126.40 million was for Grants for Battered Women's Shelters and

$3.00 million was for the National Domestic Violence Hotline. (Note: these amounts were subject to a 0.59% across-the- board rescission included in the act.) Congress also appropriated $15.00 million for the transitional housing assistance grants program as a separate line-item. Total authorized funding for violence against women programs for FY2002 was $627.30 million.

FY2003

Total FY2003 funds appropriated for violence against women programs were $519.98 million: $390.17 million for Department of Justice programs and $129.81 million for HHS programs. President Bush requested a total of $520.00 million for violence against women programs, of which $390.00 million was for programs administered by DOJ and $127.00 million was for programs administered by HHS. The Administration did not request funding for federal victims counselors or the domestic violence task force. The President requested funding for two programs that were not authorized for FY2003: safe havens for children pilot program and training programs for medical personnel who perform sexual assault forensic exams. FY2003 funding request for VAWA grants for battered women's shelters, administered by HHS, was $125.00 million, the same amount appropriated in FY2002. Authorized funding for this program in FY2003 was $175.00 million. Total authorized funding for violence against women programs for FY2003 was $627.30 million.

FY2002

In FY2002, funding appropriated for violence against women programs totaled $517.22 million; violence against women programs administered by DOJ received a total of $390.60 million, while violence against women programs under HHS received $126.62 million. Within HHS, the President requested funding for programs at FY2001 appropriations levels, and did not request monies for the transitional housing grant program created in VAWA 2000. The President also requested $44.00 million for rape prevention and Education grants; however, these grants were not specified by name in the Labor, Health and Human Services, and Education Appropriations Act of FY2002. Rather, the Administration proposed that funding for these grants be included as part of injury prevention grants. Congress provided $149.80 million for injury prevention grants. Total authorized funding for violence against women programs for FY2002 was $642.30 million.

FY2001

For FY2001, the President requested $481.00 million and Congress appropriated $407.10 million for violence against women programs, however, funding for programs created in the original act did not truly decrease from FY2000 appropriation levels. Grants to Prevent Sexual Abuse of Runaway and Homeless Youth were reauthorized in the Missing, Exploited, and Runaway Children Protection Act (P.L. 106-71) and received appropriations of $15.00 million, prior to the rescission, for FY2001. In addition, the Centers for Disease Control received $176.00 million for prevention grants such as rape education and prevention and community domestic violence programs, but the appropriations bill failed to specify amounts for the different programs. Total authorized funding for violence against women programs for FY2001 was $667.50 million.

INDEX

A

B

C

D

E

U

V

W

Y